A Practical Book for Prayerful Catechists

AND THE CHILDREN PRAY

Janaan Manternach
with Carl J. Pfeifer

AVE MARIA PRESS
Notre Dame, Indiana 46556

Acknowledgments

Scripture selections from *The New American Bible with Revised New Testament*, Copyright © 1986 by the Confraternity of Christian Doctrine, Washington, DC, are all used with permission of copyright owner. All rights reserved.

Excerpts from *Sharing the Light of Faith: National Catechetical Directory for Catholics of the United States*, Copyright © 1979 by the US Catholic Conference, Department of Education. All rights reserved.

Haiku on page 78 appears in *This Is Our Faith*, grade 7, Silver Burdett and Ginn, p. 129.

John Chrysostom, *On Matthew: Homily 50.4* cited by William J. Walsh, S.J., and John P. Langan, S.J., in "Patristic Social Consciousness—The Church and the Poor," in *The Faith That Does Justice*, ed. John Haughey, S.J. (Paulist, 1977), p. 131.

Excerpts from "Hymn of Thanksgiving," composed by Jose de Vinck, in *Byzantine Daily Worship*, Raya, ed., Alleluia Press, Allendale, NJ, 1969, pp. 399-400.

"Philip," by Harry Pritchett, Jr., *St. Luke's Journal of Theology*, vol. 19, no. 3 (June, 1976). School of Theology, The University of the South, Sewanee, TN.

International Standard Book Number: 0-87793-000-0

Library of Congress Catalog Card Number: 89-85064

Cover and text design by Elizabeth J. French.

Printed and bound in the United States of America.

AND THE CHILDREN PRAY

To
Angela and Miguel
Barbieri
Our beloved godchildren
with whom
we have
played,
cared
and
prayed.

Contents

Part Three: What Are Practical Helps to Prayer? _____ 105

Introduction

Why This Book?

During my many years of teaching religion the question that I have found the most challenging is not "How to teach?" but "How to pray?"

Many changes have occurred in my approach to children and prayer through the years, and I have grown in my appreciation of the value of and need for prayer in the lives of contemporary children. I have chosen to write this book for catechists who, like me, want to pray with children as well as teach them about God and believing.

When I began teaching religion, I always opened the class with a prayer. Later I stopped doing this, especially when I realized that I was using prayer only as a way to get the children to settle down. However, when I didn't open the class with prayer, I found that I didn't pray with the children at other times either. Frankly, for years this didn't trouble me all that much as long as I was teaching well and the children were participating seriously and enjoyably.

Then, in the '60s, I had the privilege of doing graduate study at the Catholic University of America in Washington, DC. Father Gerard Sloyan was head of the Religious Education Department and was one of the more popular professors. His classes made me take a second look at the place of prayer in the ministry of catechesis.

He insisted that all catechesis should lead to prayer. He went so far as to teach that the very purpose of religious education is to help people to pray. That, more than any of the other important things I learned from Father Sloyan, captured my imagination and led me to work intentionally at making prayer a more meaningful part of my religion classes.

Even so, my efforts were unsuccessful about as often as they succeeded. A few years later I participated in a workshop on children and prayer at a religious education congress where Carl and I were also speaking. That workshop renewed my desire to pray more with my students and made me more conscious of the importance of prayer in catechesis.

In preparing my next class I built a time of praying into it and was happy with what happened. Although I did the same thing with the preparation for the following class, one activity took longer than expected and we didn't have time for praying. I felt a pang or two of guilt about this and resolved to build praying more carefully into my next class. Again, the instructional moments eclipsed the time for prayer.

In reflecting about my failure to pray consciously with the children in those classes, I decided that I was trying to build prayer into the class experience artificially. Somehow I would have to *feel* the right time as the class progressed, pause at that moment and pray. That decision comforted me, so in planning my next class I didn't identify a specific prayer or a particular time. The result of that decision was again not praying.

My next rationalization was that my task ultimately was to instruct and that if praying happened, fine—if it didn't, fine, too. I blessed that rationalization with my belief that all of life is prayer. Now I was right back where I was before I had attended that workshop

9

on prayer and children. The only difference was that while I could rationalize well, I couldn't rid myself of the feeling that no matter how well the classes went, without prayer my religion classes were incomplete—lacking a vital ingredient.

It became clear to me that I had to find an integral way to pray with the children in each class. The prayer could not be tacked on; it had to flow into or out of what was happening in the class. It had to have the potential of bringing each of us personally, and all of us communally, more fully in touch with God within ourselves and with God's presence in others and in the created world.

That is where I am now. My commitment toward moments of prayer during my religion classes has made a difference in the overall quality of each class. I have come to believe that things happen during prayerful silence and prayerful speaking, singing, gesturing or creating—something that needs to happen to make a class a religious as well as an instructional experience.

Today I cannot imagine myself teaching a religion class without prayer of some kind. I have found, too, that preparing for class prayer times has increased my own prayerfulness. Actually, the whole effort of ministering as a catechist in the community makes more sense to me now that I have experienced over and over again what Father Gerard Sloyan taught me 25 years ago: *A primary purpose of religious education is to help people to pray.* The *National Catechetical Directory* echoes Father Sloyan's conviction in similar words: "Inasmuch as it seeks to lead individuals and communities to deeper faith, all catechesis is oriented to prayer and worship" (#145).

That is why I have chosen, with Carl's help, to write this book. I want to help other catechists discover the importance of prayer in catechesis and to develop skills at leading children to pray in and outside of class.

Another reason this book has finally come into being is the encouragement, persistence and patience of Frank Cunningham of Ave Maria Press. He never gave up on my promise to do it although there were many times when I thought it would never become a reality.

The Goals of This Book

Helping children learn to pray is closely related to one's own prayer life as a Catholic and as a catechist. We need to grow continually in our own understanding and appreciation of prayer which in turn enriches our efforts at initiating children into more meaningful prayer experiences. That is why *And the Children Pray* continually touches on our own prayer as well as the prayer of children we teach. For me the two are inseparable.

Even a prayerful catechist needs continual improvement of skills for leading children to be more prayerful, and an awareness of the many resources available for guiding children in prayer.

So I have three interrelated goals for this book: The first is to explore the question, What is prayer? Where might we look for answers? The second is to provide information on what attitudes and conditions nurture and support prayer in us and in children. The third is to suggest practical ways religion teachers can help themselves and children learn to pray.

In the process of working toward these three goals I will also recommend helpful resources available to religion teachers (and parents) that can be used in learning to pray and in teaching children to pray. They will be in a special section at the back of the book.

My deepest hope in writing this book is that you, the catechist, become more convinced of the importance of prayer in your own life and more motivated to pray often with children. I hope the many examples and suggestions I offer will help you pray more happily as you help children to pray.

Part 1
What Is Prayer?

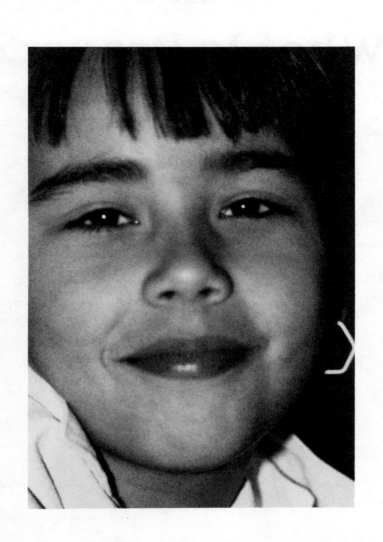

1
Drawing on Our Own Experience

What is prayer? Surely we have heard definitions of prayer from the time we were children. The one I learned long ago is that prayer is "raising your mind and heart to God." Some years later I learned another definition of prayer as "conversation with God." More recently I was struck by a much different definition of prayer as a "radical response to life."

Each of these has merit, as do many other approaches to answering "What is prayer?" We will look at old and new definitions in later chapters. But the answer to that question also needs to be deeply personal.

The definitions of prayer that mean the most to me—and that most influence my helping my students learn to pray—are those that arose out of memorable experiences of prayer that I have had over the years. For a long time I believed my definitions but hesitated to say them out loud because I discovered them in my own experience rather than in the works of great theologians or spritual writers.

Now I am convinced that we all need to look first at our own prayer experiences, trying to articulate what we have experienced. Theologians in the First World and in the Third World have, since Vatican Council II, taken this experience-based approach to doing theology and guiding their pastoral ministry. The experiences in question are not first of all those of saints and theologians, but of ordinary people who find ways to pray in their busy and alienated First World lives and in their Third World poverty and oppression.

We need to follow the theologians' example and begin our efforts at better understanding and defining prayer by looking at our own prayer experiences. Then we can test our personal definitions of prayer against the definitions of others perhaps more spiritual and learned.

15

I also believe that our personalized understanding of prayer drawn from our own experience will most guide us in our efforts to help children learn to pray. As catechists we need to be aware of our own experiences and assumptions about praying. A good place to begin is to ask ourselves, "What is prayer?" and then to delve into our own prayer experiences for a personal answer to that question.

My Experiences and Definitions

These are some of the answers that I personally have to the question, "What is prayer?" Each definition is linked to something that happened to me or in me at various times. These experiences form some of the larger road marks along my prayer journey.

One of the first experiences of prayer that I remember is relational but the relationship wasn't consciously one of God and me but of my grandmother and me. She taught me the words of the Our Father, the Apostles' Creed and other of our traditional prayers. I recited them over and over again, literally at her knees, leaning against them in comfort because they were good-sized and strong.

Those many and unhurried moments with my grandmother, who had time to go over and over the words with me until I knew them by heart, had a most lasting effect on me. Because of her love and the things that she told me about God, the receiver of these words, I found my first childhood answer: *Prayer is something you do for God with someone you love and who loves you back.* Just as it takes awhile to put together the words of a prayer so that they flow from your mouth and heart easily and surely, so does becoming a pray-er happen gradually and surely.

I love to remember another experience because it convinced me that God, though not visible, is right outside our front door as well as in our hearts. In Iowa where I grew up there were many storms accompanied by high winds, great flashes of lightning and frightening claps of thunder. When the storms were bad, my family gathered in the kitchen for comfort. That was the moment my mother would go to the front door with a holy water bottle and generously throw the water into the wind, rain, lightning and thunder.

Her gesture quieted our fear and predictably a calm would descend over the storm. I know now that by the time we had all gathered in the kitchen the storm had probably already spent itself. But I learned then a conviction that won't go away: God is someone who will calm the raging storms, inner as well as outer ones. This later childhood experience tells me *prayer is something we do that reveals to God our awareness that what's happening is out of our hands and we need help.*

Another experience happened to me as a young adult. I had graduated from high school and was teaching in a one room school in rural Iowa. I was happy there but for some reason I found myself going back and back to Cardinal John Henry Newman's prayer-poem, "Lead Kindly Light." In doing so I pondered the possibility that I was being led. Needless to say, whoever was leading did not, at the time, have a willing follower, but the poem was instrumental in my finally choosing to enter religious life. From that experience I came to believe that *praying is initiated by a God who creatively and persistently encourages a response.*

Another experience I will share took place on the day I signed the papers from Rome dispensing me from my vows as a Dubuque, Iowa, Sister of St. Francis.

I had a 2:00 p.m. appointment with the Vicar of Religious in the Chancery Office adjacent to St. Matthew's Cathedral in Washington, DC. I arrived 15 minutes early and was feeling alone, apprehensive and somewhat sad. To ease my feelings a bit and to gather some courage I slipped into a side chapel of the cathedral. Without any plan I started to pray to Mother Irmina Manternach, my great-aunt who was the Major Superior when I entered the Sisters of St. Francis. She died when I was a senior novice. I found myself praying to others of the Sisters whom I had known and whom I believed were with God. Somehow I had to have their blessing and I prayed fervently to them for courage and peace.

At two minutes to two I walked into the anteroom to the chancery offices and I announced myself to the receptionist. She informed me that I would have to wait a half hour and invited me to be seated. "I can handle the delay," I thought, "but please, God, don't let anyone I know see me sitting here." I had no sooner uttered the plea when a door opened and out walked Monsignor James Gillen, Cardinal Patrick O'Boyle's secretary. We had known each other for a long time and he had invited me to give the keynote talk at a Diocesan Religious Education Day when he was Diocesan Director.

My immediate reaction was another prayer, "O God, NO!" As he came toward me, I knew that I would have to tell him upfront why I was there. Now I suspect that he knew why I was there and had come out purposely. He could tell I was nervous and his response to my "confession" was one that is still etched in my heart and seems to have been prophetic. "That's fine!" he said, "You have done good work for the church as a sister and I'm confident that you will continue doing good work for the church."

He then sat down, motioned me to do the same and we visited in the most enjoyable way until the receptionist called me for the appointment. With that Monsignor Gillen walked with me to the elevator, told me what floor the office I was going to was on, and told me to turn left as I got off the elevator.

From that dramatic experience I learned perhaps the most profound answer to the question, "What is prayer?" *Prayer is simply being conscious of the presence of God to us in other people.*

As an aside, I feel that Mother Irmina and the sisters that I prayed to were instrumental in Monsignor Gillen's gracious appearance. Their blessing was conferred through him.

A more recent experience of prayer was more painful and profound. Several years ago Carl and I were thinking seriously about adopting a child. Our thoughts suddenly took on a note of urgency as we discovered that we might be able to adopt a specific infant about to be born of an unwed, pregnant young woman.

Our excitement grappled with our anxiety. We began to pray and to ask the advice of trusted friends and professionals.

We received completely contradictory advice from those we turned to. And the passion of their convictions tore us even more between saying yes or no to the adoption. To our surprise the State Social Services and the lawyer involved both approved us for adopting even though we were far beyond the normal age limits.

We prayed and prayed, seeking to discern God's will in what was becoming a confused, draining situation. Finally the baby was born and we had to make a decision. But our prayer had resulted in no clear answers. We made our decision to adopt, only to find one hour before we were to receive the infant that unforseen legal problems and new information about the parents ruled out our adopting that child.

We were crushed. We cried. We anguished. We prayed. As the days went on, the darkness and pain remained but we were able to fulfill our professional commitments and go on with our lives.

Cindy, a young mother and one of my many cousins, helped more than she ever guessed, by sharing a few moments and fewer words with us. Her understanding and compassion were tangible graces.

From that painful experience, which at times I felt I could never survive, I learned an adult-sized definition of prayer. *Prayer is a searching for God's will even when God seems to leave you confused, a trust in God even when you feel God may have failed you, a grasping for God's presence even when God seems absent, a heart-felt thanks for God's love felt through the compassionate eyes and touch of another.*

I could go on with more personal prayer stories that have filled out my understanding of what prayer is, but these suffice to show how important it is to look deeply into one's own prayer experiences. I've slowly learned to trust my experiences. They are touchstones I keep coming back to as I learn more about prayer from other sources.

Every catechist can benefit from similar personal reflection. Unless the definitions of prayer given by others, no matter how holy or learned, resonate with vibrations flowing from our own experience they risk remaining interesting abstractions at best, and potential deceptions at worst. The closer you are to the wellsprings of your own prayer experience as you try to guide children in prayer the more effective you will be.

Things to Think About

1. How would you define from your experience what prayer is?

2. What do you find most helps you to pray? *My Note*

3. What do you find most keeps you from prayer or interferes with your attempts to pray?

4. What is one concrete step you can take to become more prayerful during the next week?

Things to Do

1. Take a few moments to reflect on your own life. Briefly write down in story form several prayer experiences you recall. From each experience formulate a personal definition of prayer.

2. Find a quiet place and time. Relax. Breathe slowly, deeply. Pray over and over at your own quiet, rhythmic pace the plea of Jesus' first disciples: "Lord, teach me to pray." Do this only for as long as you feel comfortable with it. Then repeat the words from time to time as you go about the rest of the day. At the end of a week, jot down what you may have learned about your own praying and about what prayer is.

3. Begin a prayer journal. More or less regularly write down any experiences, insights, questions you may have regarding prayer. From time to time read over what you wrote earlier to see what you can learn about prayer from your own experiences.

2
Learning From Others' Experience

A problem with the question "What is prayer?" is that it is abstract. "Prayer" is an abstraction drawn from the varied experiences of praying people. Perhaps a better way to put the question would be, "What do prayers look like?" That way of asking the question focuses both on the people praying, the pray-ers, and on their actual prayers.

We know from our own experience how varied can be the situations in which prayers well up in our hearts. I shared some of my prayer experiences in the previous chapter. From personal prayers we can begin to develop our own understanding and definitions of prayer. We can also learn much about prayer by looking at the experiences of others.

In his book *The God Who Fell From Heaven*, Chicago theologian John Shea makes the perceptive observation, ". . . the fascinating thing about prayers is where they turn up."

Carl and I are amazed at how true that observation is. We find stories of people praying in a great variety of ways and in all kinds of situations. Frequently the secular newspapers report moving stories of people praying.

In the *Washington Post* I saw a story of a 14-year-old boy, Alex Tate, who is, to everyone's amazement, recovering from a gunshot wound he received in an altercation with drug dealers. He had been shot because he stood up to the drug dealers. He tried to get them to clear out of his neighborhood. At the end of the story is this paragraph:

His grandmother said Tate was doing fine when she visited him at the hospital yesterday morning. Just before she left, she told him that "he should praise his God every day for his life." Tate shook his head in a silent assent.

Here we might say that *prayer is praising and thanking God for the gift of life.*

In the "Style" section of the *Washington Post* several years ago, Marguerite Kelly had

20

an article titled "Parents' Almanac: Thanksgiving on Any Day." In it she suggests the value of praying.

> After a recent speech someone asked, "If you would have your family all over again, what would you do differently?" My answer surprised everyone, including myself: "Have a blessing before dinner."
> Whether you have a moment of silence, say a prayer or just count your blessings, a family needs to stop, join hands and become one. It is this circle of unity that reminds a child that he is never alone.

Prayer is a ritual that fosters community, a sense of being one with others and with God.

Cartoonists, too, often tell a story of a pray-er in a comic strip. For example, Charles Schultz has one in which Lucy is kneeling by her bed. In the first frame she prays, "And I pray that I might be a better person . . ." In the second frame she raises her bowed head and in supplication she says, "And that I will get even better . . ." In the third frame she again bows her head and continues, "And better and better and better, and. . . ." In the final frame she is sitting back on her haunches looking a bit annoyed and she says to God, "That's enough!"

From Lucy and Charles Schultz I glimpsed with a smile something of the fear we experience when we believe God may take our petitions seriously and answer them in ways we may not have expected. *Prayer is an expression of trust in God's readiness to hear our prayers, tinged with the realization that we cannot foresee or control how God will answer them.*

We can also learn much about prayer from family members, friends, neighbors, or acquaintances who share with us personal experiences in which prayer played a significant role. For example, a couple of years ago a young family who had driven here from Florida told us of this experience. The conversation had turned to religion. The young mother confessed that she no longer goes to Mass on Sundays regularly and that her faith isn't as important to her as it was when she was a child. However, she feels that religion is important and is sending their two children to Sunday School. She was convinced of its importance because, among other things, on their trip to Virginia from Florida they were in a terrible electrical storm. The rain came down in sheets and they could barely see the highway. The lightning and thunder added to the fear she was feeling. While they were in the worst of it she turned to look at the children in the back seat to see how they were doing. To her great surprise they were huddled together with their hands folded in prayer. She said that she calmed down when she saw her children praying and at the same time, the storm calmed, too. She felt sure the children's prayers kept them safe. *Prayer is a way of expressing our faith that God is greater than every evil force and cares about our well-being.*

In the spring of 1984 close friends of ours, Jim and Eileen Fitzgerald, died within a month of each other—Jim from a heart attack and Eileen when a tree fell on the car that she and her son were in during a freak electrical storm. During Eileen's funeral I was in great emotional pain and could not keep from crying, sometimes hard, during the whole service. Their children, Raymond, Molly and Patrick, were in the front pew with Eileen's brother and sister-in-law. I was amazed at how calm and controlled they were.

At Eileen and Jim's home later that day I mentioned this to Eileen's brother. He told me that as the casket was being rolled in and they were moving toward the front pew he began to feel ill and faint from the grief he was feeling. At that moment he began to pray to

Eileen, telling her that she had to help him hold up. Immediately he felt better and it seemed as though he was filled with peace. His wife and Eileen's children felt the same peaceful energy at exactly the same moment. None of them questions the effect of that prayerful cry for help and I often remember the story with awe. *Prayer binds us with departed loved ones who still care about us and can help us.*

A police officer at a meeting of religion teachers quietly shared with us that as he walks his beat he is very mindful of God's presence. He said that his prayer is one of simply walking every day or every night with God as he goes about his beat.

Sally Adlesch, my spiritual director, spends 20 minutes in prayer every morning right after she gets up. She tries just to be still in God's presence, praying over and over again the name of Jesus or another meaningful word. It's a time of almost doing nothing, allowing herself simply to be held by a loving and caring God. *Prayer is simply becoming open and attentive to God who is present always and everywhere.*

Sometimes we find real praying in those closest to us. We may learn deep lessons about prayer at home from those with whom we live. My 85-year-old mother is a good example. As long as I can remember, I remember her praying—at Sunday Mass, at family rosary, at weddings and birthdays, wakes and funerals. For years she has participated in an early morning daily Mass. She has a well-worn prayerbook filled with prayers she has collected and prayed over the years. She prays from it several times a day no matter how busy she may be.

Sometimes I do not feel in harmony with her habits of prayer or with the prayers she prays from her prayerbook. But from my mother I have learned during more years than I wish to reveal that *prayer is as much a part of Christian life as eating, drinking, sleeping or even breathing, and that prayer over the years is an expression of fidelity, of faithful love.*

We can learn a lot about prayer from others. What we learn will also influence how we guide children in the ways of prayer during our catechetical sessions with them.

Things to Think About

1. Who are some individuals you think are really prayerful people? How do they pray? What effect does their example have on you?

2. From what you know about them, why do you feel they are women or men of prayer?

3. What are some things you have learned about prayer from prayerful people, or from those who seem never to pray?

Things to Do

1. Take a few moments to think about those you feel are prayerful people, or who may have shared with you a prayer experience that touched you. From what you have observed or heard about such pray-ers, try to express in a few sentences what you are coming to understand about prayer.

2. Begin a file of prayer stories from newspapers, magazines and other sources. Clip out printed stories, or write summaries of prayer stories you have heard from others. This data may be useful in religion classes as well as for your own growth.

3. A good activity might be to gather with other religion teachers and share personal experiences of prayer. Our personal experiences will influence how we pray with our students.

3
Listening to What Children Say About Prayer

What is prayer? As we have seen, we can learn much about prayer from our own experience and that of others. A frequently neglected source of insight into prayer is the experience of children—our own children, if we are blessed with children, or those we teach.

In many ways children are the most natural and spontaneous of all pray-ers. They are so close to the freshness of life that for them, each bush is a burning bush. Every day children experience wonder and awe at realities that for adults have often become ordinary and even boring. Children respond easily to each passing joy and pain. They feel their need for some caring, powerful "other," even as they increasingly test their own self-sufficiency and independence.

So it makes sense to learn something about prayer from children, especially those closest to us. Parents and catechists, who are called to teach children to pray, need to listen to what children say prayer is.

Most children have had experiences of prayer. It is, I believe, important to find out what they know about prayer and how they experience it before we teach them more about it. I have done this in a variety of ways. One way is to invite them to fill a page with sentences that tell what they feel prayer is.

David Restrepo, a sixth grader that I taught several years ago at St. Luke's parish in McLean, Virginia, wrote the following in response to that direction.

For me and probably for most kids my age prayer is something that makes you miss the bus in the morning, or when your really tired and you want to get to sleep your mom says, "David you got to pray." I don't know. I think that praying the Our Father, and Hail Merry (sic!) etc. is alright but I don't see why you have to pray formally that way. I like praying to God my own way and saying what I feel and not what everybody else feels or not really what everybody else feels. I just want to say it my way. I know that the Our Father is a prayer that is very respectful, when I pray I am very respectful too. Oh, I do pray the Our Father, Hail Merry etc. but I do say my own prayer after I pray. You sort of get bored of praying the same thing every night and every morning.

David seems to be suggesting that *there are many ways to pray, and that even the best of traditional prayers needs to be balanced by personal, heartfelt prayers, arising within each unique personality.*

Suzy Schweiters, another sixth grader, also at St. Luke's, wrote, in answer to the same direction:

(1) Prayer is talking about God and what he wants us to do.

(2) Prayer is being silent and forgetting all your worries and thinking only about God.

(3) Prayer is good when you are down or feel the world is against you.

(4) Prayer is bad when you are in a hurry for instance: your in a championship soccer tournament and you're in the finals and on the field with five minutes left in the game and your down by one goal.

(5) Prayer is a big part of my life.

(6) Prayer is so important because some of my friends do not go to church, God listens to them and I feel he sets a good example to me.

(7) Prayer is sometimes a poem with a very beautiful picture or photograph.

Often children do not feel they know much about prayer, so I find it important to not only direct them to fill the page but to insist that they do so. For example, Suzy, above, wrote the first three statements and said that she didn't know anything more about prayer. I responded by suggesting that she could probably fill two pages with all that she knows about prayer. Grudgingly she picked up her pencil and wrote number 4. Then she looked up again and said with her eyes "NO MORE!" I focused my eyes on her and just nodded my head indicating that the page had to be filled. With that she took her pencil and scribbled on the remaining lines of the page. I simply smiled and nodded my head more firmly. After a moment's struggle she erased the scribbling and quickly filled the page with numbers 5, 6 and 7.

When she was finished she was delighted and told me that she was surprised at how much she knew about prayer. I was surprised, too.

Working with a group of third graders at Holy Trinity Parish in Georgetown, Carl and I directed them to write a paragraph describing prayer or to draw a picture. Young children often are able to say more through images than words. So we encourage them to draw as well as write their ideas and prayers. Three of the drawings by third graders are pictured here.

NAME Angela S.

DRAW A PICTURE
OF SOMEONE PRAYING.
WRITE THE WORDS OF HIS
OR HER PRAYER.

Jesus

Thank you god
for sending my father
to heaven safely
And to not
suffer any
more.

My foster sister praying
for her dad in heaven
he died. I pray for
my father that died
she is saying

DRAW A PICTURE
OF SOME ONE PRAYING.
Write the words of his
OR HER PRAYER.

NAME ___Carlos___

The drawings add much to the words, revealing more of a child's experience and feelings. Angela's drawing suggests that *prayer to God for those who have died not only helps the deceased who is with God in heaven, but also helps those who painfully miss his or her presence.*

Katy Mankin's drawing suggests a habit of nightly prayer at home. It reveals her belief that God is involved in all of life, gracious and caring for everyone, wanting all to be happy. For her, prayer might then be *thanking God for all good things and asking God's blessing on all people.*

Carlos' drawing recalls the "Jesus Prayer" that we learned and prayed earlier in that year. His drawing suggests that he has not forgotten the closeness of the risen Lord. His drawing says in image what many spiritual writers say: *Prayer is conversation with Christ, who is always with us.*

With seventh graders, Carl and I created a Prayer Profile. Leaving space or lines for answers, this includes questions such as:

> The prayer I seem to pray most often is . . .
>
> My favorite way of praying is . . .
>
> My favorite places to pray are . . .
>
> My favorite times to pray are . . .
>
> My main reasons for praying are . . .
>
> My main reasons for not praying are . . .

There are real values in giving children opportunities to describe and illustrate their experiences of prayer and what it means to them. What they write and draw reveals many surprising things. Prayers that you have introduced them to and prayed with them will show up in the drawings the way the "Jesus Prayer" did in Carlos Ferdinand's illustration. A child's attitude toward prayer will be expressed, as in David Restrepo's essay. Suzy Schweiter's list of feelings about what prayer is gives testimony to the importance of prayer in a child's life.

Perhaps the greatest value to us who are catechists is discovering that our children do pray, have owned ideas and feelings about prayer and have considerable knowledge of what prayer is. We, their teachers, can learn much from them, and the fact that we listen seriously suggests to them more than our words can that they are prayerful and can become moreso.

Things to Think About

1. What prayer experiences do you recall from your childhood, and what do you learn about prayer from them?

2. Why is it so important for us and for the children to reflect on their experiences of prayer and to articulate their ideas and feelings about prayer?

3. What have you learned about prayer from your own children or those you teach?

Things to Do

1. Adapt one of the examples given above and discover what you and your students can learn about prayer from their experiences of prayer.

2. Help your students begin a simple prayer journal in which they can describe their prayer experiences and write and collect prayers.

4
Learning From Jesus' Prayer

As our exploration of "What is prayer?" continues, we need to turn to the example and words of Jesus. The gospels give us many glimpses of Jesus praying and several of his teachings about prayer. From these gospel portraits we come into touch with the most important resource for discovering what Christian prayer is meant to be.

Jesus at Prayer

The gospels show us without doubt that Jesus was a deeply prayerful person. They take for granted that Jesus was a devout Jew, cherishing the prayer traditions of his people and being nourished by them. No doubt he learned to pray at home with Mary and Joseph, and with his neighbors at the local synagogue in Nazareth, a "house of prayer."

As a devout Jew of his time Jesus prayed in the morning, afternoon and evening. He also prayed at mealtime (Mt 14:19; 26:26). He prayed for individuals as diverse as his friend Peter (Lk 22:32) and the executioners who killed him (Lk 23:34). He prayed the psalms (Ps 22—Mk 15:34; Ps 31—Lk 23:46), observed the weekly Sabbath at home and in the synagogue (Lk 4:16), celebrated the yearly passover, and took part in temple worship (Lk 2:41; 19:45).

Jesus' ministry develops in an atmosphere of prayer, beginning with a profound prayer experience at his baptism by John (Lk 3:21-22) and ending in a final prayer as he expires on the cross (Lk 23:46). During his ministry Jesus seemed to pray anywhere—on busy city streets, at boisterous banquets, in noisy village marketplaces. But he had a predilection for quiet, solitary places for prayer (Lk 5:16)—the desert (Mk 1:35), the mountains (Lk 6:12), the seashore (Mt 4:18), an olive garden (Lk 22:39).

Jesus did not limit his prayer to the traditional Jewish prayer times. He seems to have prayed just about any time. The gospels show him praying particularly at moments of crisis or major decisions—before choosing his twelve disciples (Lk 6:12), when his initial popularity wanes (Mt 11:25), when he discerns that being Messiah means being a "suffering servant" (Lk 9:28), when he faces imminent arrest and torture (Mk 14:35), when he hangs dying on the cross (Mt 27:46).

Jesus' prayers include, according to the gospels, prayers of *praise* (of God who enables the poor and childlike to hear Jesus' message), *thanksgiving* (for God's hearing Jesus' prayers), *forgiveness* (of Peter and of his executioners, among others), *petition* (for his disciples, for all humankind), *surrender* (of his spirit to God), *trust* (of God whom he knows loves him as a son) and *confusion* (when Jesus feels on the cross that his Father has abandoned him).

Some biblical experts believe the gospels give us two glimpses into Jesus' actual prayer. One is when he realized that not only the Jewish leaders but also the crowds were turning away from him and his message (Mt 11:25-26; Lk 10:21). The other is in the olive garden when he realized he faced a violent end (Mt 26:39; Mk 14:36; Lk 22:42).

In both moments Jesus turns prayerfully to God with unprecedented intimacy and total trust. He calls God his *Abba*, his Father, in words normally used of a child to his father within the intimacy of the family circle, like daddy. His prayer reveals his unique relationship with God. He is as totally at home with God as a child with his caring father.

His other prayer-word in both painful situations is *Amen*, so be it, your will be done. Jesus surrenders himself totally to the will of his Father, whose personal love and power he trusts even in such foreboding moments.

Abba and *Amen* sum up the prayer of Jesus. In many ways that is the heart of Christian prayer: a filial conversation with God implying a readiness to accept with trust whatever God wills.

Jesus' Teachings About Prayer

Jesus' teachings about prayer echo his prayer experience. The gospels give us Jesus' teachings about prayer in a variety of settings. Nowhere do the gospels show us Jesus presenting a fully developed theory or practice of prayer. But in a number of places in the gospels we find Jesus giving us helpful teachings on how to pray. Here are some of them:

• *Pray sincerely from the heart.*   Jesus is highly critical of those who pray mechanically, multiplying words. Prayer words are not effective prayer unless they honestly express the sentiments of the heart (Mt 6:7-8; 7:21).

• *Pray without ostentation.*   Jesus criticizes those who pray ostentatiously in public so others will notice them. He recommends praying privately, aware that *God* knows you are praying. This does not mean that we should avoid public prayer, but that public prayer needs to be genuine prayer rather than a means of self-aggrandizement (Mt 6:5-6).

• *Pray honestly and humbly.*   Jesus is equally critical of those whose prayer is an expression of self-righteousness. Jesus teaches that prayer must reflect one's need and poverty before God, like the prayer of the tax collector in the Temple rather than that of the self-satisfied Pharisee (Lk 18:9-14).

• *Live as you pray.* Jesus expects prayer to be in harmony with one's life, unlike people who pray piously yet live lives of injustice, oppressing the poor and the weak (Lk 20:45-47).

• *Pray persistently.* Like the importunate neighbor and insistent widow, never give up. God cares about you and wants to assist you (Lk 11:5-13; 18:1-8).

• *Pray confidently.* God answers every prayer, even if at times he does so in ways we might not expect.

The Lord's Prayer

Jesus' basic teachings about prayer are summed up in the prayer the gospels have him teaching his disciples. There are two versions in the New Testament.

According to Luke, one of Jesus' disciples, impressed with Jesus' prayerfulness, asked him to teach them to pray the way he prayed. They also knew that John had taught his disciples a special prayer, so they wanted a special prayer as disciples of Jesus. Jesus answered with a prayer that developed into what we know as the Lord's Prayer or Our Father (Lk 11:1-4).

Matthew places a slightly more developed version of the prayer in the Sermon on the Mount (Mt 6:9-13).

The two versions reflect the traditions of two different Christian communities. Luke's version may be closer to Jesus' actual formulation, but Matthew's, more suitable to liturgical recitation, became central to the church's liturgy down through the centuries to our own time. Both share a similar content and structure.

We can put the two together, placing Matthew's developments in italics.

[Address]
> *Our* Father *in heaven,*

[First Group of Petitions]
> 1. hallowed be your name,
> 2. your kingdom come.
>   *your will be done*
>   *on earth as in heaven.*

[Second Group of Petitions]
> 3. Give us each day (*today*) our daily bread
> 4. and forgive us our sins (*debts*)
>   for (*as*) we ourselves forgive
>   everyone in debt to us (*our debtors*),
> 5. and do not subject us to the final test
>   *but deliver us from the evil one.*

The prayer Jesus taught his disciples reflects the main themes of his own prayer as well as of his teachings about prayer.

The address at the start of the Lord's Prayer shows that prayer centers on God, not on ourselves. We, like Jesus himself, are to approach God confidently as daughters and sons, calling God Father, *Abba*. We address God as *our* Father because we are brothers and sisters of the same parent. "Our Father" suggests the close link between our prayerful openness to God and a compassionate openness to other human beings. We approach God aware of our ties to others of God's children at the same time that we trust our uniquely individual relationship with our common Father.

The first group of petitions focuses on God's concerns and plan.

We pray that God act to make his holiness known and revered, as the Lord promised God's people through the prophets. We are praying that the whole world will come to recognize God's holiness and love as the source of all that is good, beautiful and lovable in human experience.

Then we pray that God act to realize God's kingdom throughout the world, God's rule of justice and compassion, love and grace—in human hearts and social structures. We pray, in effect, that God work to change the world, wiping away all tears and sorrow, hatred and division, poverty and pain, injustice and evil of all kinds, not just at the end of time, but now.

The answer to both petitions rests solely on God's gracious initiative, but God's holiness, compassion, justice and love can be realized only in people, in us. So our prayer is also a commitment, a dedication to collaborate with the Lord. We pledge to make God's plan and will for the coming of God's kingdom or reign our main concern. We commit ourselves to letting God's holiness and love, compassion and justice become obvious in how we live. We pledge to work with God in making this a better, more humane world of compassion, justice, harmony and peace.

Then, in the second group of petitions, we express our total trust in God, our Father, by expressing our own needs.

We confidently ask today—every day—for bread, food, nourishment. We pray not just for the food that stills physical hunger pangs, but the food and nourishment that fills all our human hungers: for love, happiness, community, peace, justice. In today's world, marked by widespread malnourishment and starvation, violence and war, loneliness, hatred and prejudice, alienation, oppression and injustice, with millions hungering for freedom, our prayer for "daily bread" takes on an urgent social dimension. The prayer is also a prayer for the "bread of life," the "breaking of bread," the eucharistic meal. From the earliest days of the church this prayer has been part of the Eucharist.

Knowing we are all sinners, we ask for God's merciful forgiveness. This petition is conditioned upon our own mercy toward those who have sinned against us. Matthew's "debts" and "debtors" are metaphors for "sins" and "sinners." God's forgiveness comes to us through our own forgiveness of others.

Finally, in a world beset with all manner of temptations and evils, we pray to the all-powerful God for protection and deliverance. We pray for God's help not to give in to temptation, not to bow before the forces of evil in everyday life and to be victorious with Christ in the final struggle between God and the Evil One at the end of time.

The Our Father or Lord's Prayer is *the* prayer of the Christian disciple. It sums up Jesus' own prayer life and his teachings on prayer. The risen Lord gives us his Spirit, the Holy Spirit, to help us pray as Jesus taught us.

What we learn about prayer from Jesus' example and teaching is vital to our own prayer life and to our catechesis.

Things to Think About

1. What did you learn about prayer from Jesus' example and teachings?

2. What do you find most challenging about Jesus' example and teachings about prayer? Why?

3. In what areas of your life do you sense the greatest tension or dissonance between your prayers and your lifestyle?

4. To what extent are your prayer priorities in harmony with those of the Our Father?

Things to Do

1. Re-read the chapter with your bible at hand. Look up each of the biblical references given in the chapter. Read and ponder each text, letting your imagination picture each scene, seeing Jesus and any other people involved, hearing their words, sensing their feelings. Express any prayers that rise up in your heart.

2. Occasionally, pray the words of the Our Father very slowly, one at a time. Spend a moment or two meditating on each word. Notice your feelings and any new ideas or perspectives on the meaning of the words. End by praying the whole prayer through in your customary way. You may pray any familiar prayer in this way.

3. Make for yourself some creative reminders of the core of Jesus' prayer, the two words *Abba* and *Amen*. For example, use crayons or paints to make an attractive sign or poster, carve the two words in wood, paint them on smooth rocks, shape them from clay, embroider them, illustrate them with magazine photos. Place the completed reminder in a place where you will see it during the day.

5
Learning From Mary's Prayer

What is prayer? For centuries Christians have turned to Mary as a model of prayer. For many Mary is *the* faithful disciple of Jesus and therefore *the* model of prayer for all others who follow her Son. We would do well to turn to the gospels to explore what we find there about Mary's prayer life.

Except for Luke's gospel and its sequel, the Acts of the Apostles, little data about Mary's prayer is to be found in the New Testament. And most of that is found in the first two chapters of Luke's gospel. These chapters, the "infancy narratives," are carefully constructed theological interpretations rather than historical documentaries. Luke constructed them with an astute eye on the Hebrew scriptures, our Old Testament.

But his literary constructions about Mary must have rung true to early Christian communities as fitting the woman they knew as Jesus' mother. So we may cautiously draw from them some idea of Mary's prayer life as Christian tradition has sketched it. For centuries, millions of Christians have modeled their prayer on the biblical portrait of Jesus' mother at prayer.

Luke presents Mary first as a young Jewish girl living in a small hill town in rural Galilee. Her life and her prayer are typically Jewish, drawing their content and style from the Hebrew scriptures and traditional Jewish practices. Undoubtedly she prayed faithfully as all devout Jews of her time three times a day—morning, noon or early afternoon and night—as well as at mealtimes, took part in the local synagogue services, and observed the sabbath rituals at home as well. She would have known and prayed by heart many of the psalms and other biblical prayers, as well as traditional blessings.

Luke mentions two visits to worship in the Temple in Jerusalem, first as she and Joseph presented the infant, Jesus, to God (Lk 2:22-40), and again when Jesus was about 12

(Lk 2:41-50). She and Joseph may even have travelled once yearly to Jerusalem to join in the temple worship.

Our first glimpse into Mary's actual prayer in Luke's gospel is perhaps the most basic and suggestive. We have come to know the experience as the Annunciation (Lk 1:26-38). At the time Mary is a teenager growing up in Nazareth. She is betrothed to Joseph, a village carpenter. Soon they are to be married.

One day Mary mysteriously experiences God's call to her to become the mother of the Messiah. She is understandably amazed and puzzled. Why me? How can this be? How will I know for sure?

But then, totally trusting in God's word to her, she surrenders to God's will. "I am the servant of the Lord. Let it be done to me as you say." Her trust-filled act of faith echoes the faith of millions of the *anawim*, or "poor ones" of her people, women and men of all positions in life, but mostly those who knew economic as well as spiritual poverty. These poor ones in the Hebrew scriptures were those who could not trust in their own strength and recognized their need to trust in God. They were mainly the poor, lowly, hurting marginal people in Israel, the "widows" and "orphans." The psalms are the prayers of these poor ones. In contrast, the rich are not those who are affluent but those who place all their trust in themselves and sense no need of God.

Mary and her Magnificat echo the psalms and the spirit of the *anawim*. We see in Mary's prayerful acceptance of God's will that this traditional spirituality of the poor was to become central to the prayer experience of those who follow Mary's Son. That same surrender to God's will must be central to the prayer of all Jesus' disciples: "I am the servant of the Lord. Let it be done to me as you say." "Father . . . not my will but yours be done." "Our Father . . . thy kingdom come, thy will be done."

Mary's relative, Elizabeth, praises her for just this openness and fidelity to God's will in Luke's description of Mary's hurried visit to share the good news with Elizabeth and to support her during her pregnancy (Lk 1:39-56): "Blessed is she who trusted that the Lord's words to her would be fulfilled."

In response to Elizabeth's song of praise and welcome, Mary sings her Magnificat. Known also as Mary's Song this remarkable composition provides us with a traditional summary of Mary's prayer, much as the Our Father sums up Jesus' prayer. We will take a closer look at it after filling in further details of Mary's prayer life as Luke paints it.

The story of Jesus' birth in Luke reveals another key to Mary's prayer (Lk 2:1-20). Luke mentions that after the shepherds came to see her newborn son, "Mary kept all these things, reflecting on them in her heart." Luke indicates in similar words Mary's prayerful response to the painful experience of losing Jesus in the Temple when he was 12 years old (Lk 2:51). She "kept all these things in her heart."

This treasuring, pondering and remembering apparently was a traditional form of biblical prayer. It involved sensitive reflection on the experiences of daily life together with remembering or keeping in mind how God dealt with people in the past as recorded in the Hebrew scriptures. Mary pondered God's mysterious action in her life in the light of God's saving actions in the history of her people. Luke seems to suggest that such prayerful reflection permeated Mary's life. Out of the quiet pondering came prayerful expressions of thanks, praise and other deep responses to God.

Luke's final mention of Mary comes after the Ascension of her triumphant son. In the midst of Jesus' other disciples, Mary spends her days in constant prayer in the upper room in Jerusalem (Acts 1:14). She was apparently with them on the feast of Pentecost when they experienced the coming of the Holy Spirit.

Luke portrays her now as a disciple of Jesus in the midst of his other faithful disciples. In fact Mary, alone among the disciples, is the living link with Jesus from his conception in Nazareth to the church's birth in Jerusalem. He may be suggesting what the church today realizes, namely, that Mary is the first disciple of her son and the model of Christian discipleship.

At the church's beginning we see Mary praying in the community of disciples. Her prayer arises within the community and is nurtured by the community, just as her example of prayer nurtures the community. This final image of Mary suggests that prayer, while intensely and intimately personal, finds its natural context and nurture within a prayerful community.

The gospels do not provide us with more than these few glimpses into Mary's prayer life. Yet what they suggest about Christian prayer is vital, and very similar to what we have learned about prayer from the gospel portrait of Jesus at prayer.

Mary's Song: Magnificat

The longest prayer found on Mary's lips in the New Testament is the Magnificat or Mary's Song (Lk 1:46-55), which Luke records during Mary's visit to Elizabeth. From New Testament times the church has held this Marian prayer in special honor, praying it each day during Evening Prayer (Vespers). Christians have come to view it as a summary of Mary's prayers and thus as a model, along with the Lord's Prayer, of how Christians are to pray.

It is not likely that Mary actually prayed this prayer as Luke wrote it. It seems rather that Luke adapted a Jewish-Christian prayer already part of the Christian community and placed it on Mary's lips as she responded to Elizabeth. The Magnificat clearly reflects the prayer of Hannah, the mother of Samuel (1 Sm 2:1-10) and was probably created after the resurrection within the Jewish-Christian community. Luke attributed it to Mary—a common practice in the Bible of placing words in the mouths of important persons—because it fit so well his own image of her. The early Christians who knew Mary must have found it fit her well or they would not have been comfortable with Luke's attribution of it to her.

> My soul proclaims the greatness of the LORD;
> > my spirit rejoices in God my savior,
> For he has looked upon his handmaid's lowliness.
> > Behold, from now on will all ages call me blessed.
> The Mighty One has done great things for me,
> > and holy is his name.
> His mercy is from age to age
> > to those who fear him.
> He has shown might with his arm,
> > dispersed the arrogant of mind and heart.

He has thrown down the rulers from their thrones
    but lifted up the lowly.
The hungry he has filled with good things;
    the rich he has sent away empty.
He has helped Israel his servant,
    remembering of his mercy,
according to his promise to our fathers,
    to Abraham and to his descendants forever (Lk 1:46-55).

First Half: Individual Praise and Thanks.   The first five verses of Mary's prayer-song are a beautiful hymn of praise and thanksgiving to God. Mary recognizes everything about herself and her life as God's gift. God is the source of her joy. The great God looked at her, a "lowly" servant. Yet she will be called blessed because of the great things the mighty God has done for her. God alone is holy and unchangeably compassionate to those who open their hearts to the Lord.

I remember hearing these words and praying them with heartfelt thanks to so gracious a God from the time I was a child. They sum up my traditional image of Mary as a beautiful young woman totally aware that her goodness and beauty are God's gift. St. Augustine echoed the spirit of Mary's prayer several centuries after New Testament times: "We are lovable, Lord . . . because you have loved us!" The words of Mary's joyful song of praise have been put to music by countless great composers—moreso than any other texts from the Bible. The many beautiful musical compositions by some of the world's greatest composers (Vivaldi, Palestrina, Mozart, Berlioz, Bach and others) reinforce the positive, calm, comfortable, joyful, consoling, affirming sentiment of the words of the Magnificat.

Second Half: Social Cry for Justice.   Curiously I have paid considerably less attention to the second half of Mary's prayer. So has the church in which I have grown up and worked for many years. The second half is disturbing, puzzling, challenging. Mary seems to be praying that what God did for her personally reflects what God wills for all. The individual pattern of her life—God singles out a poor country girl in the backwaters of the Roman Empire to raise up to a greatness unequalled by even the emperor, Caesar— exemplifies a broad social pattern of God's plan.

Mary sings that God confuses and scatters the proud, deposes the mighty, sends away the rich with nothing, but gives good things to the hungry and raises up the lowly to high places. It is a puzzling pattern of reversal reflecting a radical re-evaluation of society's typical values. Mary echoes the great Hebrew prophets of old—Hosea, Amos, Isaiah, Jeremiah, Ezekiel—who spoke out in the name of God who sides with the poor, oppressed and weak.

And she expresses what the gospels show her Son doing—seeking out the downtrodden and marginal people of Galilee and Judea. Jesus' beatitudes, especially in Luke's version, express even more dramatically the challenging reversal of values in what makes people happy or blessed: "Blessed are you who are poor . . . woe to you who are rich; . . . Blessed are you who are now hungry . . . Woe to you who are filled now; . . . Blessed are you who are now weeping . . . Woe to you who laugh now" (Lk 6:20-26). Jesus tells several parables with the same message: the rich and powerful are put down and the lowly and poor are blessed, for example, the stories of Lazarus and the rich man (Lk 16:19-31), of those invited to a banquet (Lk 17:7-10) and of the rich farmer (Lk 12:16-21).

Along these lines the Vatican affirms that "a theology of freedom and liberation as a faithful echo of Mary's Magnificat, preserved in the memory of the church, is urgently needed in our time" (*Instruction on Christian Freedom and Liberation*, #48).

Mary's Song is worth praying and pondering, both its comforting, mystical first half and its challenging, prophetic second half. From the gospel portrait of Mary at prayer we get a surprisingly rich insight into what it means to pray as a disciple of her Son, Jesus Christ.

Things to Think About

1. What images come to mind when you think of Mary praying?

2. How closely does your own prayer reflect the themes and attitudes of what the gospels suggest about Mary's prayer?

3. Why do you feel the Magnificat is a favorite prayer of people in First World countries like the United States and Europe? Why is it also one of the favorite prayers of the poor in Third World countries of Latin America, Asia and Africa?

Things to Do

1. Assemble for yourself and for use in your classes a broad collection of images of Mary, including those of Mary at prayer. Consider them with your students, either to encourage them to find in Mary a prayerful model, or to compare/contrast the images of Mary praying with the gospel portrait of her prayer life, or to add visual support to meditation or a slide-sound presentation. For example, select a musical version of an *Ave Maria*, or *Magnificat*, or other Marian hymn and set selected slides of Marian art with the music.

2. Look up the Magnificat in your bible (Lk 1:46-55). Using the notes and cross references in your bible look up the texts they refer you to. In this way you can discover how the Magnificat echoes many passages from the Hebrew scriptures and the New Testament. You might have your students do this with you.

3. Invite your students to write modern versions of Mary's Magnificat, with the same number of verses as Mary's but in words that more directly express her thoughts and feelings in contemporary words and images.

6
Learning From Christian Tradition

What is prayer? Christians have some 20 centuries of prayer experience. We need to look at that rich spiritual tradition as we continue to explore the meaning and ways of prayer. Needless to say our sketch of some 2,000 years of praying will be shamelessly superficial. But, hopefully we will be able to arrive at a modest but helpful summary of at least some major threads of the rich and diverse fabric of Christian prayer.

Regular Prayer Times

Christians shortly after New Testament times tried to make their whole lives a prayer. That was the goal described by Clement of Alexandria in the second century. The perfect Christian lives his or her life in God's presence.

Making your life a prayer was no easier then than now. Clement, Hippolytus and Tertullian tell how the early Christians worked at this. They prayed regularly at certain times: on rising in the morning, before meals, at the third, sixth and ninth hours, before going to bed, and even during the long nights. (These "hours" are not identical with our clock hours; for example, the "third hour" would be the third hour after sunrise, not 3:00).

The prayers prayed at these regular prayer times varied. Writers mention especially the Our Father (evening) and Creed (morning) and brief biblical prayers. Hippolytus suggests recalling at the other hours the sufferings of Jesus that took place at those hours (third: crucifixion; sixth: Christ prays aloud on cross; ninth: piercing of Christ's side). Others suggested recalling Jesus' resurrection each morning upon arising and his second coming each evening on retiring. In this way, as Hippolytus put it, "in every event you keep Christ before your eyes."

41

Christians soon found a need to come together for prayer even though they prayed regularly in their homes. From New Testament times the Sunday Eucharist was the central prayer experience of the Christian communities. Ignatius of Antioch describes how all the Christians living in a town or surrounding countryside met together on Sunday for the Eucharist.

Other community prayer developed for weekdays. Hippolytus mentions occasional prayer meetings during the week, but the practice really developed after the church became official in the Roman Empire. Eusebius of Caesarea in the East and Hilary of Poitiers in the West reveal how universal the practice was in the fourth century. Augustine mentions how his mother, Monica, regularly went to church each day in the morning and evening.

Each morning and evening Christians living close enough to the cathedral or other church gathered for community prayer. They recited psalms together, sang hymns and prayed aloud. Sometimes there were readings from the Bible. Sometimes there was a homily. But always there were one or more psalms, hymns and prayers. In this way many Christians came to know by heart the psalms that were used most often at the daily prayer services. Undoubtedly they prayed these psalms by heart during the day as they went about their lives.

Constant Prayer

While it seems most Christians tried to pray faithfully at the specified times, especially morning and evening, at least in their homes, and to take part in Sunday Eucharist and the weekday morning and prayer meetings at church, some Christians felt called to a life of more constant prayer. Epiphanius writes of his and others' efforts to "pray without ceasing." Living as hermits devout men and women learned ways of praying in their hearts as well as in words. Anthony became the most famous of them. Athanasius' popular fourth century life of Anthony reveals some of the hermits' approaches to prayer. They learned to keep their hearts on God as they worked, weaving mats, for example, by repeating over and over a brief prayer, like "Help me," or "Have pity on me," or the name "Jesus." The "Jesus Prayer" became one of their best loved prayers and is being discovered anew by many contemporary Christians.

Liturgy of the Hours

Meanwhile, other Christians were drawn to more prayerful lives in community. They lived a common life in neighborhoods near a martyr's shrine or a basilica. There were such communities of lay persons and priests in Jerusalem and Caesarea already in the fourth century and in Rome a century later. These groups prayed together seven times a day, adding two new "hours" to the three customary private prayer hours—third, sixth, ninth—and the morning and evening prayer services in church. Thus developed what we know as the "divine office" or "liturgy of the hours." The "hours" were made up of psalms, followed by a biblical reading, hymn and prayer.

Similar arrangements of the prayer hours were found in the monasteries that were growing up outside the cities. The goal of constant prayer embraced by the hermits was now pursued by monks and nuns in community through the regular prayer of the "hours" together. The psalms dominated their group prayer, with some monasteries praying the entire 150 psalms each day!

Biblical Reading and Reflection

Benedict put a lasting stamp on monastic life in the sixth century. Benedictine monks and nuns filled the day with the communal "divine office," balanced with manual labor, and individual "divine reading." The latter was a meditative, prayerful reading of the scriptures. Jerome became the greatest advocate of such scriptural reading and prayer. The influence of the monks spread this way of biblical meditation beyond the monastery walls. Unfortunately few outside the monasteries could read and bibles were almost non-existent.

The lasting value of such biblical meditation and prayer is being rediscovered today by many Christians who take quiet time to *read* a biblical text, *reflect*, ponder, meditate on it, and *pray* in response to it.

Our knowledge of prayer among lay people in the villages of medieval Europe is very limited. We know that the Irish made up repetitive prayers that could be easily memorized. The "Breastplate" of St. Patrick is one of these that remains popular. We know, too, that devotions to Mary, saints and angels multiplied as theologians focused more on Jesus' divinity and on people's sinfulness, and as the liturgy became more and more distant from the average lay person, who no longer knew Latin.

Prayer books were written for the relatively small number of educated noblemen. The average layperson could not read and at most may have known a few verses from a few popular psalms. Their prayer life probably centered on the repetition of prayers, particularly the Our Father, and brief "ejaculations" like, "Have mercy on me, O God," with repeated gestures like genuflecting and prostrating. Most probably also knew and prayed the Creed. They also joined in lengthy litanies, responding after each invocation, "Lord, have mercy."

Popular Devotions

About the 11th century a new breeze of spirituality refreshed the church. Christians began to focus more concretely on Jesus' humanity. Christians were moved at the thought of Jesus' birth and utterly anguished at the image of his passion and death. Christmas and Good Friday took on new meaning.

Devotions developed to honor Christ's wounds. Pilgrimages to the Holy Sepulchre became popular. The Hail Mary now became one of the most popular prayers. All Catholics were soon expected to know it along with the Our Father and Creed. Hymns like the "Hail Holy Queen" multiplied to honor Mary. There were various litanies of Mary. And then came the Rosary.

The Rosary became the people's psalmbook. Earlier it had become common for the laity to substitute 150 Our Fathers for the 150 psalms prayed by the monks. By the mid-12th century 150 Hail Marys became more popular, soon broken down into three sets of 50. About a century later "mysteries"—events in the lives of Jesus and Mary—were suggested for meditation while praying the Hail Marys. Devotions to saints were also popular.

Francis of Assisi and Bernard of Clairvaux had a profound influence on the spirituality of Christians in the 13th century. Both stressed devotion to Jesus Christ as a personal response to a Savior who shared the full range of human pain and suffering. Francis created the creche so believers could visualize the infant in his crib. He likewise drew popular attention to Jesus' five wounds. He seems to have composed two popular prayers that are still loved: the Canticle of the Sun, and the Peace Prayer. Francis and Bernard urged people to contemplate the events of Jesus' earthly life and to imitate him in their own lives. They also spread a deep love of "Our Lady."

Bonaventure and other Franciscans developed meditations on the life and passion of Jesus. They encouraged people to use their imaginations to enter more fully into the meditations.

Mystical Prayer

About a century later a vibrant mystical movement spread from some monasteries to people outside. Members of the new Dominican order, notably John Tauler and Meister Eckhart, spread this new mysticism through their preaching and writings. Gertrude the Great drew many to set their hearts on mystical union with the heart of Christ. Even more popular, Julian of Norwich wrote an important book on God's love drawn from her mystical experiences.

The Franciscans, Dominicans and other new orders had a profound impact on the prayer lives of the laity through their Third Orders. Members often prayed from popular Books of the Hours, filled with psalms and other prayers. They read spiritual and devotional books like lives of Christ and lives of saints. Besides Sunday Mass—attendance at which was now obligatory—the prayer life of most Christians centered on devotions to Mary and saints, processions for feasts like Corpus Christi, religious plays, including Passion Plays, and the recitation of the Our Father and Hail Mary. These popular devotions had little relationship to the church's liturgy, which people could neither understand nor participate in.

Mental Prayer

Lay persons in the newly emerging cities of the 14th and 15th centuries, able to read and reasonably well educated, increasingly turned to mental prayer. They often joined together in groups to support one another in their lives of prayer. They worked out a weekly schedule of prayer and prepared notes for meditation, mostly on the life and sufferings of Jesus. They developed methods of mental prayer, with hints on how to prepare, how to meditate, how to pray in conclusion. The most popular and lasting of the books they created was the *Imitation of Christ*, which many Catholics still find helpful.

This emphasis on mental prayer found great support in the life and work of Ignatius of Loyola and the Society of Jesus which he founded in the 16th century. His *Spiritual Exercises*, to be experienced during retreats of varying lengths, remain very influential. He set out several methods of mental prayer and devoted most of the exercises to meditations on the life, death and resurrection of Jesus. Mental prayer more and more became a part of the daily life of all monks, religious communities and devout lay persons.

Ignatius moved religious life from a monastic mold to a more pastoral one. He exempted his Jesuits from the communal praying of the Divine Office and encouraged a form of contemplation firmly rooted in apostolic action. He felt prayer was to be integrated into daily life and centered on love and imitation of Jesus Christ.

About the same time John of the Cross and Teresa of Avila were also calling people to a life of mystical union with God. Francis de Sales, a bit later, taught another simple method of mental prayer. His *Introduction to the Devout Life* became and remains very popular. It stresses God's love and presents a positive attitude to the world and to human nature, recognizing beauty and appreciating life's pleasures. Not much later, Brother Lawrence of the Resurrection made popular a simple method of "practicing the presence of God" throughout the day.

More Popular Notions

After the Council of Trent and the Reformation in the 16th century, Catholic piety continued to develop practices of mental prayer and popular devotions. Aside from frequent reception of confession and communion, popular prayer remained separated from the church's public liturgical worship. There was a new reverence for the Blessed Sacrament with the development of Benediction and Forty Hours. Jean Jacques Olier began the practice of frequent "visits" to the Blessed Sacrament in the 17th century.

There were a growing variety of novenas and triduums. Processions, religious plays, litanies of all kinds became very popular. Many new prayer books contained a wealth of prayers for all occasions. Meditation manuals appeared, with detailed directions for how to meditate.

John Eudes and Margaret Mary Alacoque popularized devotion to the Sacred Heart, and later added the Heart of Mary. Louis de Montfort pushed devotion to Mary to an extreme. He urged Catholics to do everything in, for, with and through Mary, becoming her slaves.

Needed Reform

The church that many of us grew up with in the present century prior to Vatican Council II reflected the devotional practices of the 16th, 17th, 18th and 19th centuries much more than the church's earlier prayer traditions. We were at home with vocal prayers like the Rosary, devotions to the Sacred Heart, Mary and the saints, Benediction and Forty Hours, frequent confession and communion, days of recollection, retreats and mental prayer. Much of the devotional life we knew had little or no relation to the scriptures or to the church's official worship and scarcely reflected the hierarchy of beliefs we professed in the Creed and learned in the catechism.

The Second Vatican Council in the 1960s led to a reform of Catholic prayer practices in the light of the church's long and rich spiritual tradition. Today, in many parishes, Catholics experience the community celebration of the Eucharist each week as a central prayer experience. They find their own prayer nourished on the church's traditionally central resource for prayer, the Bible. Catholics today experience a renewed call to mystical union with Christ and an equally urgent call to express their prayer in serving those in need and working to transform the world into a more hospitable, just and peaceful place for all people. Christ is the central focus of Christian prayer, while devotion to Mary remains important, and prayer to the saints is being reborn after a couple decades of neglect. Many Catholics are finding renewed spiritual value in the Liturgy of the Hours, prayed privately or in a group. They are becoming once again familiar with the Holy Spirit. Most recently the deep wells of spirituality among the poor of Third World countries is beginning to nourish First World Christians.

Conclusion

It is important for us catechists of children to realize, even from so sketchy an overview, how rich a prayer tradition we have as Catholic Christians. Our students have a right to be exposed to a healthier, sounder, more balanced and traditional prayer life than many of us grew up with. And we need to enrich our own prayer lives with some of the rich spiritual practices we may not have been exposed to earlier.

Our Catholic prayer tradition includes:

• *vocal prayers* of all kinds from traditional prayers like the Our Father, Hail Mary, and Creed to simple, oft-repeated words or phrases, to blessings, to litanies;

• *mental prayer*, from meditative reading, through meditation, simple prayer, to contemplation, opening out to the highest reaches of mysticism yet permeating the most energetic pastoral action;

• *centering prayer* like the Jesus Prayer;

• *popular devotions* of all kinds;

• *prophetic prayer* expressed in efforts at social justice, peace and world transformation;

• the church's official *liturgical prayer*, including the Eucharist, the other sacraments and the Liturgy of the Hours.

We have a wealth of ways of praying *together* or *individually*, of praying with the *Bible* or other *spiritual reading*. We have ways of praying with *one word*, with *short phrases*, or with *no words*; ways of praying *in any place*, *at any time*, and *in a variety of positions*. We can pray prayers of *praise* and *adoration, love, thanksgiving, sorrow* and *intercession*, as well as *petition*. We have *traditional prayers* coming down through the centuries and *newly made prayers* meeting the needs of our time, and *never before expressed prayers* uttered spontaneously as the Spirit urges.

To reduce such a wealth of prayer experience to a neat definition seems foolhardy, but Christians have from time to time tried to articulate their prayer experience. Underlying the various definitions is the awareness that ultimately *prayer is a response to God's gracious presence in our lives moving us toward closer contact and union with that Presence.* God speaks a word to us, a call, an invitation, a challenge. Prayer is our response, our effort to enter into more intimate dialogue or conversation with God who speaks to what is deepest in our hearts. In a life-changing, *radical response to life*, we *raise our minds and hearts to God*, entering into *conversation with God, resting in God's presence*, to paraphrase some common current definitions of prayer.

One of the better definitions of prayer we've found is in the *National Catechetical Directory* in its treatment of prayer and catechesis:

> At the very heart of the Christian life lies free self-surrender to the unutterable mystery of God. Prayer, for both individuals and communities, means a deepening awareness of covenanted relationship with God, coupled with the effort to live in harmony with His will (#140).

The rest of this book will relate these prayer insights into the practical catechesis of children, drawing upon some of these ways of praying.

Things to Think About

1. With which of the church's prayer practices do you feel most comfortable? Which are most meaningful in your life?

2. Why do you think Catholic prayer experiences have changed so much over the centuries and continue to change?

3. What basic threads do you recognize running through these 20 centuries of Christian prayer practices?

Things to Do

1. Take a highlighting pen and reread this chapter. Highlight any prayer practices you are not familiar with. Single out one or two of these that seem more interesting to you. Find out more about them and see how you might incorporate one or more of them in your prayer.

2. Look at the prayers in the religion textbook you are using this year. List them all and if possible make a copy of all of them on one or two pages. See to what extent they reflect the richness of Catholic traditions of prayer. Learn these prayers yourself as the weeks go on and pray them yourself.

3. Take a pen and a blank sheet of paper. Fill the paper with sentences that tell the story of your personal prayer life—what was it like when you were a child? an adolescent? a young adult? What is it like now?

Part 2

What Nurtures and Supports Prayer?

7
Looking for God in All Things

I'm not quite sure when or how I became conscious that God is everywhere and connected with all that is. I do know that I knew it before I learned the answer to the Baltimore Catechism question, "Where is God?"

I suspect it happened to me in infancy. At whatever stage of development I discovered my mother, father and others of my family, I probably discovered another whose name is God. Prayer and church were always central to my family's lifestyle, therefore God was as much a part of its totality as was everything else. God was blessed and thanked for any and all of the good things that happened in our lives. When we were worried, anxious or afraid, we placed the situation in God's care. When we were in need, we cried out to God for help, and whatever came about to change things, we identified with God's action for us. If some thing of beauty made us catch our breath, we uttered a prayer of praise. Even what was ugly was perceived as some thing that God wasn't finished with yet, or as somehow having the potential for being redeemed through God's loving power.

I believe this attitude is mostly acquired. And, the earlier children are put in touch with the presence of God in all things, especially people, and learn that God is present and acting in all events, the surer we can be that it will be a part of who and what they are.

Children, especially young ones, can readily believe in the endless possibilities of God's presence. With their imaginations they delight in the discovery of God's closeness to them in the whole of life.

Gerard Manley Hopkins writes in one of his famous poems that "the world is charged with the grandeur of God." To awaken children to this profound yet simple awareness is, I believe, the responsibility and challenge of parents, grandparents, godparents, clergy and

51

religion teachers. Actually the whole community of faith might gift our young with this kind of rootedness in God.

This awareness and wonder in children and young people will be revealed at surprising times. I was surprised by its presence in one of my nieces during a phone conversation. Kim was 16 at the time. She has always spent a lot of time with my mother, her grandmother, who perceives everything that is and that happens as somehow flowing out of God's care and connectedness to all of life. As part of our phone conversation Kim kept going back to a tragedy that had occurred near her home the night before. Two young people had been killed in a car accident. While Kim was telling me about it she kept interjecting the question, "I wonder what God is doing in all of this?" I finally asked her why she thought God had anything to do with the accident. She immediately responded, "I know God is a part of everything that happens but when it's bad I always have a hard time figuring out how." I was surprised and pondered a long time over that conversation because up to that time I was unaware that Kim related events to God's presence and activity.

There are numerous opportunities every day and in every situation to help children to look for God in everything and to acknowledge it. One of the traditional keys to growth in prayer is learning, as St. Ignatius Loyola put it, to "find God in all things."

God's Presence in Themselves

Children need to learn early to sense God's loving presence with them always. Prayers acknowledging God's ever-present love for them not only lead to praise and thanks, but also reinforce self-esteem. The more children come to believe that they are loved just because of who they are, the better they may become.

For example, in relation to a child's discovery of a new talent, or to some accomplishment, we might teach the child a brief biblical prayer like Mary's song, "My soul proclaims the greatness of the Lord; / . . . The Mighty One has done great things for me" (Lk 1:46;49), or the prayer of St. Augustine, "I am lovable, Lord, because you love me." Or the children may make up similar spontaneous prayers or write prayers.

When facing a difficult challenge, we can teach a biblical prayer like: "God is our refuge and our strength, / an ever-present help in distress" (Ps 46:2), or "But for me, to be near God is my good; / to make the Lord God my refuge" (Ps 73:28). There are many similar brief prayers in the Bible. You and the children can also make up this kind of prayer.

In this way we help children sense that their very being, their talents, their strength, their dreams and expectations, are all signs of the gracious presence of God within them. Dr. Thomas Francoeur, a Canadian psychologist and religious educator, believes that God is so close to children that he figuratively describes this mysterious reality in the poetic language of the psalms: "God holding them in the palm of his hand." Our task is to help the children grow in this prayerful awareness.

Psalm 139 gives perhaps the classic biblical expression to this realization.

> O LORD, you have probed me and you know me;
>   you know when I sit and when I stand;
>   you understand my thoughts from afar.

My journeys and my rest you scrutinize,
    with all my ways you are familiar.
Even before a word is on my tongue,
    behold, O LORD, you know the whole of it.
Behind me and before, you hem me in
    and rest your hand on me.
Such knowledge is too wonderful for me;
    too lofty for me to attain.

Where can I go from your spirit?
    from your presence where can I flee?
If I go up to the heavens, you are there;
    if I sink to the nether world, you are present there.
If I take the wings of the dawn,
    if I settle at the farthest limits of the sea,
Even there your hand shall guide me,
    and your right hand hold me fast (Ps 139:1-10).

A similar awareness of Christ's presence within and about us is found in the lovely prayer known as the "Breastplate of St. Patrick":

May Christ shield me today . . .
Christ with me, Christ before me, Christ behind me,
Christ in me, Christ beneath me, Christ above me,
Christ on my right, Christ on my left,
Christ when I lie down, Christ when I sit,
Christ when I stand,
Christ in the heart of everyone who thinks of me,
Christ in the mouth of everyone who speaks of me,
Christ in every eye that sees me,
Christ in every ear that hears me.

God's Presence in Things

Children in our society, especially those in more affluent families, grow up with so many things that they may readily take things for granted, both natural resources and the products of technology. From early on we need to help them appreciate things, use them with respect and see them as signs of God's goodness and presence in all things. Not only does this open up their hearts and minds to God's presence everywhere, but it fosters a respectful attitude to all of creation—the environment, natural resources, science and technology.

Another Canadian religious educator, Francoise D'Arcy-Berube, has spent much of her life helping parents and teachers sense possibilities for helping their young grow in this awareness of God's presence in all things. She suggests, for example, that, while watching a beautiful sunset with children or looking at a flower in new bloom with them, we praise and thank God for it together. We can do the same as youngsters pause in awe at the marvellous intricacy and intrigue of a modern computer game, the product of God-given creativity at work with God-given material resources. Without waiting for an awe-inspiring sunset, we can have the children look around the room and name the signs of God's presence and love that surround them.

A traditional way the church has of linking things with God is the use of blessings. Blessings do not make ordinary things holy. Rather by blessing an object we acknowledge its inherent goodness as a creature of God, and ask God to continue to be with us as we enjoy or use it. We recognize and affirm its reality as created and held in being by a gracious ever-present God, whose presence can be discerned through all created things. Blessings help us focus our eyes on specific things as "small-s" sacraments.

We can involve children in the blessing of pets, bikes, books and computers, homes, cars, food and drink, of anything that has importance in their lives.

A most meaningful blessing is the family blessing of car keys. As each child turns 16 and is able to drive the family car, parents and other members of the family gather around the potential new driver. The parents speak of the big step one of the family is about to take—the privilege of driving. They speak of the responsibilities involved. Then the parents pray a homemade blessing over the car keys as they give them to the new driver. That blessing is simple but impressive. In a family of seven children where this was an ongoing ritual, none of them were ever injured or injured any one else while driving.

Perhaps the most common and potentially meaningful blessing for children and adults is at mealtime. Few practices can have so deep and lasting an effect on children's prayerful awareness of God's presence in their lives as the regular experience of "grace at meals" at home and, where appropriate, at school or class. And, even though shared meals in many families today are neither regular nor common, when they do happen, prayer should be a significant part of the event.

In addition to the traditional Catholic meal blessings, parents, teachers and even the children themselves can compose appropriate meal prayers. Here is one our godchildren learned in school and prayed for several years with us or their parents each evening before dinner as all held hands:

> God is great, God is good,
> and we thank him for our food;
> From his hands we all are fed.
> Give us this day our daily bread. Amen.

When we visited their Honduran grandparents, we noticed this meal prayer hanging on a plaque above their table:

> *Bendice, Señor, los alimentos que vamos a tomar;*
> *Dános salud para ganarlos,*
> *paz para disfrutarlos,*
> *y amor para compartirlos. Amen.*

> Lord, bless this food which we are about to eat;
> Give us health to work for it,
> peace to enjoy it,
> and love to share it. Amen.

I especially love the ancient Jewish and Christian practice of the blessing cup. It is particularly meaningful at special family meals, and can also be used in class with lunch or snacks. The family or class selects or buys a special cup or goblet to be its blessing cup, and keeps it in its own special place.

When used at a special meal, snack or lunch, a designated person pours wine, or juice, into the blessing cup. She or he then raises it and thanks God for some blessing, takes a sip from the cup and passes it to the person on the right, who does the same ritual and passes on the cup. When the cup returns to the person who raised it first, he or she prays a closing summary prayer. All may sing a hymn or song if desired. The blessing cup ritual is a beautiful way for children within a family or other community to grow in prayerful awareness of God's presence in the things and events of life.

The blessing cup book named in the Bibliography, page 186, is a very helpful guide for this kind of prayer before meals.

God's Presence in People

Obviously blessings and the blessing cup may be used to praise and thank God for people as well as things. Parents may bless their children, who in turn may bless their parents and one another. Catechists, too, may bless their students, especially on special occasions. In this way the children can become more aware of God's presence with them in and through others.

Some blessings may be taken from the Bible, like the one Moses passed on to the Israelites (Nm 6:24-26):

> The Lord bless you and keep you!
> The Lord let his face shine upon you,
> and be gracious to you!
> The Lord look upon you kindly and give you peace!

Others may be taken from the liturgy, like the Solemn Blessing used during Advent:

> May God make you steadfast in faith,
> joyful in hope, and untiring in love,
> all the days of your life.

Even the common liturgical blessing used at the end of the eucharistic celebration may be used:

> May Almighty God bless you,
> the Father, and the Son, and the Holy Spirit.

Or you might prefer using an ethnic blessing like the old Gaelic blessing:

> May the road rise up to meet you.
> May the wind be always at your back.
> May the sun shine warm upon your face,
> the rain fall soft upon your fields,
> and until we meet again
> may God hold you
> in the palm of his hand. Amen.

Perhaps even more meaningful to a child is a blessing you create yourselves for special occasions. The family might work together to write an appropriate blessing, or one member might pray a spontaneous blessing prayer, using words that arise out of the heart at the moment.

Children learning about the beatitudes and the commandments can be given significant glimpses of people who lived their lives in such a way that God's presence and action were very visible in who they were and what they did. Perhaps looking carefully with children at great and heroic people who treated others and things with radical care and respect is the best way to help them discover and believe in God's presence in people in their lives.

An obvious way of helping youngsters become aware of God's watchful and caring presence in the lives of people is by teaching them to pray for people—at bedtime, at mealtimes, on special occasions. The general intercessions prayed at the Eucharist provide a helpful litany formula for praying for people. It might be adapted for use at home or in class.

God's Presence in Church

The Catholic church so believes in the presence and self-communication of God in all created reality that its chief rituals are celebrations of this fact. Actually the church as a whole is the sacrament of Christ's presence in the world. The seven sacraments each celebrate Christ's involvement in a vital dimension of human experience using symbolic actions and elements from daily reality.

Looking closely at the sacraments is a significant way to open children's minds and hearts to God's presence in themselves and in others as well as in bread, water, fire, oil, breath, wind and gesture. Times of sacramental preparation are particularly precious times of helping children look for God's presence in all of life.

Preparing young children for their first communion is an ideal time to guide them in experiences of thanking God for all the gifts and people that are in their lives and to look for and become aware of new things and people in their expanding relationship with their families, their church, their neighborhood and world. They can also be helped to see in the church's concern for the suffering the healing presence of Christ in the world.

Fifth grade provides another excellent opportunity to foster this sense of looking for God in all reality since it is often devoted to a more in-depth study of the seven sacraments and the church's many sacramentals.

Confirmation preparation, often during junior high or high school, offers another good time to help open our youth to God's presence in their often confused world. They particularly need moments simply to rest in God's presence. Guided imagery meditation can be very effective at this age. So can meditation using strong photos or art, or carefully selected music. In these ways the young can be helped to look for God in their own worlds of meaning.

Carl and I often use music as background for centering and imaging activities, guiding the youngsters in a personal affirmation of God's presence in themselves, others and things.

What often amazes me about junior high students and the quest for God is that on the one hand they will profess a complete lack of knowledge and a great deal of doubt, while on the other hand they enter into prayer readily with both ease and enthusiasm.

Perhaps what Dr. Thomas Francoeur says about young children having a natural sense of God's presence is as true of older children. If not as apparent, perhaps even latent, it does exist and perhaps accounts for why most children enter into experiences of prayer, especially those that remind them that God is with them and that God's face is visible in all that is.

A haiku poem speaks of the kind of awareness that can be nurturing and deepening for this age.

> Your presence is like
> Warm sun, soft rain, yellow rose—
> Nurturing new life.

Such are but some of the rich variety of ways we can help children look for God's presence in every aspect of their lives.

Things to Think About

1. How committed are you to looking for God yourself?

2. How much do you really believe God is present in your life, in the whole of creation?

3. In what people, things, experiences do you most find God?

4. From whom did you learn to look for God in all creation? Who supports that faith search in you now?

Things to Do

1. Look up Psalms 8 and 139. Take one at a time. Read the psalm slowly, becoming sensitive to its feelings as well as its images and ideas. Note any words or images that most move you. Learn by heart a verse or two that you feel at home with and comfortable praying. Pray it from time to time every day.

2. Think of your own experience of God's presence and/or absence in your daily life. Then write a psalm or other prayer expressing whatever sentiments you most feel about God in your life.

3. Find or make an hour during which you can be free to take a quiet walk alone. In a relaxed way try to notice many signs of God's presence in the world that opens itself to your senses. Without strain *look* for signs of God's presence in the world you normally rush through preoccupied with work or worries. Perhaps take a camera with you to capture some of these signs on film for later prayer.

8
Openness

For me, prayer comes naturally. Almost anything will lift my mind and heart to God. A homeless person, the first crocuses of spring, headlines of a devastating earthquake, the children in my religion classes, our godchildren, Angela and Miguel, a card or letter, a loaf of bread, a bottle of wine, a meal with friends, sickness, the participants in a workshop, a good book, a good movie, a senile parent, an aging but well one.

This has always been so for me. I remember, as a child, praying as I was walking to a one room schoolhouse in rural Iowa, and later, as a teacher there, doing the same thing.

Openness to God, which is related to our efforts to look for God in all people and things, depends upon an abiding belief that God is. It also depends upon an expectancy and a certainty that God cares passionately for us, that we are unconditionally loved and that God is for us at all times and in every situation. I believe, further, that openness to God happens in the ordinary ongoing development of a person from infancy into childhood, adolesence, young and older adulthood.

As an infant is cared for and becomes aware and open to people who smile and cuddle; as a child reaches toward someone he or she trusts and enjoys; as a child explores his or her environment and is fascinated by it, he or she is developing a personal openness to all that is, which includes God as creator, God as parent, God as the ground of all being.

Whatever happens to the environment of a child at home, at play or in school increases or decreases his or her practice of including and acknowledging God in the everyday business of living. The more a child feels comfortable in the world with its people and things, the more room he or she will have for God who lives there also.

Catechesis plays a significant role in the growing openness to God that is possible in children. God needs to be named for children, not just at home, but in formal teaching and liturgical settings. God's story needs to be told to them over and over again. And the mystery of believing without tangible evidence needs to be entered into with children. They question and will introduce their wonder if given a chance, and many times unexpectedly.

When Angela, our goddaughter, was nine, we were chatting in the car on the way to ballet class. I was about to pay for the next semester's classes which amounted to over a hundred dollars. I told her what the classes cost and suggested that it required some sacrifice on our part, but that the sacrifice was lovingly made. Just for fun I then asked her who else loves her so much that they make great sacrifices for her. She named her parents, her teachers and several others. I continued to question, asking her if she remembered someone who loves her so much he sacrificed his life. She thought for a moment and then said, "Jesus" but added, "I don't really know him though because I've never really met him." She then wanted to know how you could know someone that you had never really met.

Thinking fast, because she had just been with her family in her father's home town near Kansas City, Missouri, I reminded her that she knows her grandfather and many things about him because her daddy told her stories about him when they visited where he lived and worked. And, I reminded her that she had never met him. With a big sigh of understanding she answered, "Oh, that's how you know people you've never met." Then she added, "I was just kidding, I really do know Jesus."

In planning my religion classes I spend time on what might happen to the inner environment of each of the students during the lessons. My biggest challenge is to design the class so that each one becomes involved, that some fascination is stirred up, that some questioning occurs, that some acceptance takes place and that some praying happens. Openness depends upon those things. When a parent tells me that her child really enjoys the classes and wants to come, when there are fewer and fewer absences as the year goes on, and when a genuine feeling of friendliness exists between them and me, then I feel that I have developed a greater openness to God—not only in each of them but also in myself.

A climate in the class that develops openness to God is not solely dependent upon the preparing and actual teaching and exchange that occurs between the students and me and among the students themselves. In great part it depends upon peripheral things such as chatting a bit with a child when he or she arrives, asking a child to go to the office with you to pick up some materials, giving a child the task of checking off attendance, remembering a comment or a question asked at random by a child and bringing it up later, fitting it significantly into what is being discussed. The latter takes practice but is not all that hard to do and can win over even the most reluctant religion student. Winning children over is part of the task of increasing their openness to God.

Many opportunities in religion classes enable us to introduce children to an attitude of openness to God and inspire them to be personally open to God. Particularly helpful are stories from the Bible. For example, in the story of Abram going forth from the land of his kinsfolk to a land that God would show him, Abram went as the Lord directed him, open to the Lord's guidance, into an unknown future (Gn 12).

The story of Moses is another example of someone a bit reluctant, perhaps, but ultimately trusting, opening himself to the Lord's call (Ex 3, 7—14).

Other stories include the revelation to Samuel and his response, "Speak, for your servant is listening" (1 Sm 3:10), Judith's utter confidence in God's presence and plan (Jdt 8: 9-27), the story of Job, probably one of the most intense and surprising examples of complete openness to God (Job 42:1-6). The prophets are particularly good examples of openness to the call of God. When God called Isaiah, asking "Whom shall I send? Who will go for us?" Isaiah responded without hesitation: "Here I am; send me!" (Is 6:8). Jeremiah, however, was more fearful, more reluctant to accept God's call. "Ah, Lord God! . . . I know not how to speak; I am too young" (Jer 1:6).

In the New Testament we again have numerous examples of openness, such as Mary who willingly became mother of the mysterious Messiah (Lk 1:38), Joseph, who took Mary as his wife even though the child she was bearing was not his (Mt 1:19-24) and John the Baptist, who agreed to baptize Jesus although he felt that he should be baptized by Jesus (Mt 3:14-15). The disciples who answered the call to follow Jesus had to be open to leaving all things behind (Mt 4:18-22). Zacchaeus (Lk 19:1-10) and Mary Magdalen (Jn 20:11-18) are two others who are remembered for their openness to the Lord. Finally there are the people who asked for and received healing from Jesus (Mt 8:5-13).

In introducing children to these people I focus their attention on the attitude and spirit of openness that is revealed and pray with them for the same spirit and attitude of openness in themselves.

Praying much and often is probably the greatest key for helping children to be open to God's call, God's presence and action in their lives. The more opportunities children have for prayer the more their relationship with God will grow. The deeper their relationship is, the more open they will be.

Things to Think About

1. What have you experienced as opening you to life, to other people, to the world around you, and more consciously to God?

2. What in your life do you feel tends to close you to God's presence?

3. Why is it so hard at times to remain open to God and God's will for you?

Things to Do

1. Take a few minutes of quiet, uninterrupted time to reflect on your lifestyle, looking closely at the past six months or year. Notice people or things that tend to keep you locked within a safe, comfortable existence. Sense any long-standing inner dreams and ideals that your daily routine closes you to. Try to discern what would make you more open to your better self, to others and to God.

2. As you plan your next lesson, take some time to think of one small, concrete step you might take in that class to help the youngsters be more open to life and to God. Think about their lives. What factors and forces in their daily lives tend to close them up, make them superficial, keep them from being more open to God?

3. Look up in your bible one or more of the stories referred to above. Try to identify with the person, his or her situation, feelings and decision to be open to the Lord's will. Then pray to become more like that person in your own day-to-day living.

9
Thankfulness

When Angela, our goddaughter, was eight she was invited to a birthday party, a sleepover. Before the party she thought a long time about a gift for her little friend and selected one that she was very excited about. Unfortunately her excitement gave way to sadness and confusion during the party itself.

The crisis began when the birthday child and the other guests took some of the candy that Angela was saving to take home to her little brother. This hurt but then they also hid from her, which confused and hurt her even more.

When Angela returned from the party the next day, she didn't want to talk about it until all of a sudden she started to cry, spilling out the whole story between sobs.

Thinking I might distract her by getting her to remember what I was sure was a happy moment in the party, I asked how her little friend liked her gift. That only made her cry more as she kept wailing, "She didn't even say thank you. I think she liked it but she didn't thank me at all."

I felt sad because her little "friends" had shut her out during the party until a parent intervened, but what made me feel like crying along with Angela was the additional pain she felt about not being thanked for a gift she had chosen so lovingly and carefully.

Angela's friend failing to say thank you could have been a simple oversight in a context where a lot was happening all at once; however, even young children know that the words, thank you, can be more than just an expression of gratitude. They can be building blocks in a growing friendship. "Thank you!" can be an affirmation of the gift giver's thoughtfulness. It can also be a sign saying to the gift giver, "You know me because you chose something that you were sure I would like."

To say thank you is often a gracious way of saying "I love you."

Children will be thankful if they are taught to be that way. An example: Several years ago I was teaching a sixth grade class and I quickly became aware that most of the children ignored gracious gestures on my part and on the part of their peers—gestures like picking up something that had fallen and returning it to the owner, pouring an extra glass of juice or offering an additional cookie. Early in the year I had wrapped and given each one an autographed copy of the prayerbook, *Living Water: Prayers of Our Heritage*, which Carl and I have written. Only two of the children said thanks.

That troubled me! Actually, like Angela, I cried that evening as I was falling asleep because I felt they had taken my gift for granted. But mostly I felt something special, something deeply human was not very well developed in most of these children.

Thanksgiving was coming up in three weeks so I decided to start teaching them the importance, the value and the need for thankfulness, not only in their personal lives, but in the lives of those who care about and are constantly doing loving things for them.

In the next class I told them of a Thanksgiving Plan. Using the holiday as a jumping off point helped. I began by asking them to make two lists—one naming people who love them so much they are always doing both necessary and unnecessary things for them, the other list naming people who do caring things for them on special occasions like birthdays or Christmas. That was easy. Most of them named parents, brothers, sisters, grandparents, godparents, other relatives, friends and a few named a teacher. I also made a list of my own.

I then reminded them that Thanksgiving was coming up, a perfect time to say thank you to people who are caring, helpful and thoughtful of us.

I suggested that we each look silently at our lists and choose two people to thank in a special way on Thanksgiving Day. I gave some hints about ways to say thank you—through a letter, a poem, a small gift. The important thing was to do it thoughtfully and with affection. I promised that I would also do it and that during the class after Thanksgiving we would share what we had done and tell how it had gone.

After Thanksgiving we did that. Not all the children had remembered to do something. One said she had chosen not to. And that was okay.

Right after Thanksgiving I suggested again that many people, especially members of our families, spend a lot of time trying to figure out what gift would make us really happy at Christmas time. They try to remember things that we've expressed a desire for and feel might be a wonderful surprise. They do this because they love us and want us to have a delightful Christmas.

I then told them that they are old enough to do something as caring, old enough to show appreciation for all that's done for them through a gift that they made or bought with their own money. I also suggested that this time they choose their parents and that it should be more than a gift—it was to be their own personal way of saying, "Thanks, Mom, thanks, Dad, for all the things you do for me all year long."

I kept emphasizing the gift-giving as something deeper than just handing someone a present.

After Christmas we remembered again what we had done. This time no one had forgotten, no one had chosen not to do it and three of the children said that it was the best part of Christmas for them. Needless to say I was delighted.

I also had noticed that when I had handed each one a small gift during the last class before Christmas, each one had said thank you in an appreciative way. It made my day!

We did something similar for Valentine's Day and again at Easter. But the most memorable thing happened on the last class of that year.

Each child—every single one of them—brought me a gift to say thank you—a plant, a card, a bouquet of fresh flowers (two of the boys had gone together for it), a book, a poem, a letter, a heart pendant. Several of the mothers were so awed by what was going on that they phoned me afterwards to tell me that they had had nothing to do with the gift-giving. Two of the mothers stopped by toward the end of class because they wanted to be part of it all. They couldn't believe their children, on their own, had orchestrated a thank you shower.

I came home from that class, put the gifts on the living room floor, sat down and wept. Carl came down from his office to see what was the matter. I told him that nothing was the matter but I was just overwhelmed with what the children had done, with the way they had said thank you. I added, "You know, I think I not only helped them to become thankful little people, I feel I've also humanized them in a much deeper way." He looked at me for a moment and said, "I think they've also added much to your humanness."

That, perhaps, is one of the most gracious things that has ever happened to me in my long teaching career and, I believe, one of the best.

To help children become more consciously and carefully thankful is to help them become more eucharistic. *Eucharistia* is the Greek word for thanksgiving and praise.

The inner movement of thankfulness in a child deepens his or her potential for communion with God, with Jesus Christ and with others. For when children are genuinely and demonstrably thankful, they reveal a sense of what it means to receive, to be sacrificed for, to be loved.

I personally believe that words of thanks are the most prayerful of all words. In prayer, these words are usually ones of praise. Even a superficial reading of the psalms confirms this. Over and over one finds the same theme of thanksgiving and praise building to a crescendo through the 150 psalms:

> I will give thanks to you, O LORD, with all my
> heart (9:2).
> Sing praise to the LORD, you his faithful ones,
> and give thanks to his holy name (30:5).
> I will thank you always for what you have done (52:11).
> I will give thanks to you among the people, O LORD,
> I will chant your praise among the nations (57:10).
> I will praise the name of God in song,
> and I will glorify him with thanksgiving (69:31).
> We give you thanks, O God, we give thanks (75:2).
> I will give thanks to you, O LORD my God,
> with all my heart (86:12).
> It is good to give thanks to the LORD,
> to sing praise to your name, Most High (92:2).
> Let us greet him with thanksgiving;
> let us joyfully sing psalms to him (95:2).
> Be glad in the LORD, you just,
> and give thanks to his holy name (97:12).

Give thanks to the LORD, invoke his name (105:1).
Give thanks to the LORD, for he is good (106:1; 107:1).
Let them give thanks to the LORD for his kindness (107:8,15,21,31).
I will give thanks to you among the peoples, O LORD (108:4).
I will give thanks to the LORD with all my heart (111:1).
Give thanks to the LORD, for he is good (118:1,29).
I will give thanks to you, for you have answered me
and you have been my savior (118:21).
Give thanks to the LORD, for he is good (136:1).
I will give thanks to you, O LORD, with all my heart . . .
I will worship at your holy temple and give thanks to your name (138:1-2).
I give you thanks that I am fearfully, wonderfully made (139:14).
Sing to the LORD with thanksgiving (147:7).
Let everything that has breath praise the LORD! Alleluia (150:6).

Jesus grew up with the psalms. It is not surprising then that he exemplifies thanksgiving in his own prayer and in his teaching. The scripture story in which Jesus cures the ten lepers and only one returns to say thanks, suggests how important Jesus felt gratitude is. He asked the grateful one sadly, "Ten were cleansed, were they not? Where are the other nine?" (Lk 17:11-19).

Since being thankful is a learned response, children need to hear and feel it happening in their homes and classrooms and on the playground. They need to be thanked consistently for things they do and say.

Angela, from the time she was very small, quickly noticed a festive table, pretty earrings, an attractive dress or tie, a bouquet of flowers and she would express her admiration, to which we would respond, "Thank you for noticing" or we would simply hug her and tell her thanks.

Now when something she has done or is wearing is appreciatively noticed, she spontaneously says thanks.

When she and Miguel, her brother, are given a gift, no matter how small, they will not only say thanks immediately but will also express their gratitude with a big hug.

In great part Angela and Miguel are as thankful as they are because their daddy believes that the gesture of giving thanks is very important and is one he wants his children to learn. He also is a deeply gracious person.

Being appreciative is part of who and how Angela and Miguel are. However, they are not so spontaneous nor conscientious about writing thank you notes to their Uncle Paul and their aunts—Bernie, Sister Angela Rose and Tia Odeth—who are in other states and always send them Christmas and birthday gifts. That's because we, the adults in their lives, haven't made sure that they thank people they can't touch and see as well as those who are where they are.

I have discovered over the years after giving many children many things, that not too many have been taught to say thank you through writing. However, this year has been an exception. After giving gifts at Christmas time to three children that I have grown fond of, I first received a loving note from their mother which she closed with, "Please receive the thanks of a grateful mother's heart." Then, from each of the children came the following notes.

Dear Janaan,
Thank you for the lovely decoration book. Everything in it is so beautiful! It was the only thing I got this Christmas that I can work with and create with. It is much appreciated; it will bring hours of fun.

Love, Rachel

Dear Janaan and Carl,
Thank you very much for the calendar. I will be sure to use it. It was a very generous gift. Thank you.

Love, David

Dear Janaan and Carl,
Thank you for the game. I haven't played it yet but I'm going to play it. It looks fun. One more thing I hope you had a merry Christmas.

Love, Jonathan

Also, at the end of our last religion class before Christmas one of our fourth graders shyly handed us the following note of thanks:

Dear Mr. Pfeifer and Mrs. Manternach,
Thank you for being my Sunday school teachers. Merry Christmas.

Chris Menges

When Carl and I work with parents whose children are going to receive first communion, we spend time during the sessions encouraging parents to seize opportunities for forming the attitude of thanksgiving in their children as part of preparing them for receiving the Eucharist.

There are many opportunities in religion classes besides doing a thank you project with them. In almost every class, when I pray with the children, the word *thanks* is woven into the sentiments we're praying.

At times I have guided the children in dramatizing the story of Jesus and the healing of the ten lepers. I have had children who are one of the nine who don't express gratitude get so into it that they ask if they can go to Jesus and thank him even if the nine in the story didn't.

As in everything that will potentially develop the human and religious spirit of children, the adults in their lives, both parents and religion teachers, need to grow in the attitude themselves and be convinced of its necessity in creating and nurturing children of prayer.

Things to Think About

1. To what extent is your own prayer marked by gratitude to God?

2. How readily do you express sincere gratitude to those who do you a favor, give you a gift, or help you in some way?

3. How conscious are you of fostering in your children and in your students a sense of gratitude and skills at expressing thanks to God in prayer and to others in word and deed?

Things to Do

1. Share with the children some of the psalm verses that express thanks to God. Let them each select one they like best. Ask them to learn the verse by heart and pray it often. Suggest that they make a banner or poster or other art form containing that psalm verse, and put it at home where they and their family will see it often.

2. Pray with the children the Byzantine liturgical prayer, *Hymn of Thanksgiving* (see page 157). Then invite them to make a picture prayer book, using each couplet as the text for a two-page spread, illustrated with photos or original drawings. An alternate would be a slide-sound or video presentation in place of a book.

3. Make a note on your lesson plans for a month reminding yourself to show gratitude openly and often to the children, and to help them deepen their sense of gratitude and increase their skills of expressing thanks.

10
Reverence

Reverence is closely related to awe, yet there is a difference insofar as awe happens spontaneously whereas reverence can be taught and is a learned response. Reverence is an expression of deep respect or regard for a person or thing in recognition of its inherent worth and beauty. Reverence is also closely related to wonder. "Building upon the sense of wonder, catechesis leads people to a sense of the sacred and to recognition of God's presence in their lives" (*NCD*, #145).

Reverence is vitally important content in the rearing and educating of our children. Reverence for people and things assures that they will be treated with concern and care. It is the basic attitude behind struggles for human rights, particularly nonviolent strategies and tactics. Reverence for self translates into a good self-image, a deep sense of self-worth, which can be a deterrent to depression and suicide, and can be a source of motivation for utilizing personal gifts and talents. Reverence for things can prevent the destruction of the environment and assure the proper treatment of the living and non-living creatures that God gave to human beings to care for and use.

A reverent person is, by that fact, a prayerful person in the deepest sense that he or she senses a presence, a power, a value in persons and things that transcends their lovely, awesome, yet fragile existence.

How can we teach children to be more reverent and therefore, more prayerful?

Reverence, Respect, Wonder

Rachel Carson, whose groundbreaking environmental writings center on wonder, respect and reverence, provides parents and teachers with a challenging response to that question.

A child's world is fresh and new and beautiful, full of wonder and excitement.

It is our misfortune that for most of us that clear-eyed vision, that true instinct for what is beautiful and awe-inspiring, is dimmed and even lost before we reach adulthood. If I had influence with the good fairy who is supposed to preside over the christening of all children I should ask that her gift to each child in the world be a sense of wonder so indestructible that it would last throughout life, as an unfailing antidote against the boredom and disenchantments of later years, the sterile preoccupation with things that are artificial, the alienation from the sources of our strength.

If a child is to keep alive his inborn sense of wonder without any such gift from the fairies, he needs the companionship of at least one adult who can share it, rediscovering with him the joy, excitement and mystery of the world we live in (*The Sense of Wonder*, pp. 42-45).

Self-Respect

I believe that the first and foremost way to teach children reverence is to treat them respectfully and reverently. When we revere children just the way they are, they can learn to value and thereby revere themselves. Only then will they be able to revere others.

I have discovered that to be true in many instances in my teaching career. Two instances are etched in my memory, both times with sixth graders.

Kenneth was a most troublesome child and I was never sure of what he would do next. But the thing that most gave me a sinking feeling in my stomach was when he would simply crawl under the table in response to a question or a direction. This would bring the class to a complete halt and I would feel undone as the rest of the class looked at me with the question, "What are you going to do now?" I made up my mind that Kenneth would be above the table with the rest of us or we would all be under the table with him. I chose the former as more workable and did everything I could to bring this about, being sure not to diminish Kenneth in the process. It was hard going but together Kenneth and I negotiated and gradually he became comfortable, even productive. At times he surprised all of us with his observations and participation and none of this went unnoticed.

The classroom space was really an office, and one evening after class toward the end of the year Kenneth was helping me put the office back in order after the others had gone. We were both in a hurry so we weren't chatting until Kenneth broke the silence with the statement, "Mrs. Manternach, you're different!" My immediate silent reaction was, "Ouch!" because I was afraid of how he might find me different. Before I could respond he continued, "You think I'm all right!"

I often remember that moment with awe and gratitude.

The other time was with Pamela. She walked to class and usually arrived before the others so we talked until the others came. One time Pam came in really looking down. I asked her if she were all right. She glumly said, "Yes." I knew better so I asked her if she wanted to talk about it. She said, "No!" and tried to assure me that she was fine. I suggested that she didn't look fine to me. With that she blurted out that one of the girls in her class had invited everyone but her to her birthday party. In an attempt to help her deal with the pain, I asked her why she felt she wasn't invited. I was shocked with the reasons she gave—every one suggested to me that if she had been the one inviting, she wouldn't have invited herself.

There were many instances in which Pam revealed that she didn't have much respect for herself, so I made a concerted effort to help her see herself differently.

Gradually I began to detect a difference in things she said about herself and her situation. For example, before one of the classes, she announced that her teacher hated her. But, after thinking about what she had said, she quickly added, "You know, it's not just me, he hates everybody."

One of the biggest signs of a change in how she was seeing and accepting herself came in February. We had looked at the film strip "Phoney Baloney" which is about the Publican and the Pharisee praying in the Temple. Following the viewing, I had the children do a worksheet on which they drew an image of the scene that most impressed them and wrote a paragraph about what they would always remember from the story. This is what Pamela wrote:

> I feel it was an excellent story and that it was very easy to understand. It will always stick with me and I will turn to the fact you don't have to be fabulous to pray.

Reverence or respect for each child can be fostered in still other ways. Few actions suggest one's regard for another as clearly as listening to him or her. How we listen to each individual can convey the genuine respect we have for her or him.

Eric Hoffer, the longshoreman-philosopher, was cared for by a Bavarian woman after his mother died. He recalls the impact she had on him because she listened. Here are his recollections:

> And this woman, this Martha took care of me. She was a big woman, with a small head. And this woman, this Martha, must have really loved me, because those eight years of blindness are in my mind as a happy time. I remember a lot of talk and laughter. I must have talked a great deal, because Martha used to say again and again, 'You remember you said this, you remember you said that . . .' She remembered everything I said, and all my life I've had the feeling that what I think and what I say are worth remembering. She gave me that . . . .

Respecting Others

Similarly teachers can foster children's respect and reverence for one another by insisting that they really listen to each other when sharing ideas. In class it is typical for children to distract themselves while another child is speaking. We adults can give our children a lifelong gift by helping them learn skills of listening that manifest an attitude of respect for the person speaking.

Here is a technique that I have used successfully with children in getting them to listen carefully to each other. Before they share, for example, their answers to several questions on a worksheet they just completed, I have them write down a vertical line of numbers on the left hand side of a sheet of paper (or on the back of the just completed worksheet), one number for each child in the class beside themselves. Then, while the first of the children shares his or her answers, the other children listen carefully, and note down after the #1 on their lists anything they actually learn from the first child's answers that they did not know before. Then they do the same after #2 on their lists as the second child shares, and so on until all have responded. After the sharing is completed, each shares what new things he or she learned from the others. By doing this from time to time the children begin to appreciate that they can learn by listening to one another, thereby growing in respect for each other.

To treat children consistently with respect and reverence can be personally demanding. It requires reflection on how each child acts during the classes and a way to build this into the planning for each lesson. An example: One year I was teaching religion to 27 third graders at Fort Belvoir, Virginia. Several children in the class were repeatedly disruptive and none of the things I did seemed to make a difference. Several times I blew it by acting out angrily not only at their behavior but at each one, personally. I would feel really guilty after those classes but, on the other hand, I felt they deserved what they were getting. The sad part was that it wasn't working.

That was how I found out how valuable are dramatizations in "soothing the savage beast" not only in the children, but in myself as well.

While the children were involved in being other than themselves as characters in the dramas, they discovered potential for being respectful, for being interested, for participating wholeheartedly, for being reverent.

Practicing Christmas playlets or other kinds of dramatizations are often perfect opportunities to suggest ways of acting that reveal reverence. Children easily and quickly adopt an attitude of reverence in specific situations and characterizations.

Dramatizations provide exercises in owning or taking unto oneself the qualities possessed by someone who was reverent toward self, others and things. It also provides opportunities for telling the children what being reverent means.

In planning dramatizations I ponder how a part could be acted out by a particular child and envision outcomes. Needless to say, this approach doesn't always work, but it works often enough that the results began to show up in all aspects of the classes. A child who receives affirmation and applause for doing something positive and worthwhile most likely is rewarded enough to give up negative and disrespectful behavior.

Spending time planning each child's apparent needs and personality into each religion class is as important as the time spent on how to teach the content. Granted the latter is much easier and less time consuming, also more controllable, but the greater payoff can come in becoming more and more skilled in the former.

How children are handled, which means how they are spoken to, how they are listened to, what reactions they experience, what expectations they feel, and how cared about and appreciated they are, teaches them how to be the same way to others. These things are the hallmarks of a reverent, respectful person.

Children should never be allowed to use violence against each other, which also means violence should never be used against them. This is true for home, classroom, playground and social situations.

Hitting another with words, hands, feet or objects is what I mean by violence in this instance. The more children hear and learn in every situation that this kind of behavior is unacceptable, the greater are their chances for learning a respectful and reverent way to deal with situations of conflict, situations that ignite anger, seem unfair or encroach upon rights.

Reverence for Things

Reverence needs to extend to things as well as to people and self. Particularly for children growing up with an excess of material goods in an affluent country reverence for things is vital. Widespread lack of respect for natural resources presently endangers the quality of life on planet earth.

I believe proper respect for things can be taught or at least enabled in children. Our own respect for the things we have, enjoy and use gives the youngsters a model of reverence that they can emulate. Not allowing neglect, misuse or destruction of things in your classroom is another practical step for fostering a healthy respect for the world and its resources. Training in skills of using things carefully and enjoying things happily also helps.

Teachers can foster respect for things by insisting that the children use materials and equipment carefully and properly, do papers and projects neatly, clean up their workspaces and cooperate in leaving the classroom clean and orderly. Such "housekeeping" chores are of a piece with fostering the basic respect or reverence for things that is an important attitude for prayer.

But I have found one of the most effective means of encouraging respect for created reality among children is to surround them with beauty. I learned this through my experience of teaching in an impoverished inner-city school in Chicago. When I arrived there, I could hardly stand my classroom. It was dark and dreary. The youngsters absorbed and reflected some of the depressing environment.

Gradually as the year went on, first they, then I, became conscious of the ugliness of the room and its effects on us all. So we worked together to make it a place of beauty. We brought in flowers. We hung up colorful pictures and posters. Eventually we were able to get the classroom repainted with brighter colors. We introduced music, song, drama, poetry and children's books.

The children changed as the weeks passed. Their classroom became the loveliest place in their lives within the "concrete jungle" in which they lived amidst the city's violence and drug culture. They began to take care of their room, their desks, their clothes, their work, themselves. Now, more than 20 years later, I still hear from some of those children whom beauty touched so powerfully.

"Beauty," as psychiatrist Rollo May says, "is not God, but it is the resplendent gown of God and of our spiritual life." Centuries ago, medieval theologian Thomas Aquinas put the same insight into the language of his philosophy. He saw beauty as one of the "transcendentals," one of the human realities in which God's attractive presence becomes most visible and tangible. And centuries before that, Plato taught that beauty is "the splendor of the One showing through the Many." Modern scientists and mathematicians increasingly echo this ancient insight today.

The perception of beauty was long considered to be important in fostering a life of goodness, truth, harmony. My experience confirms the transforming power of beauty in the lives of children. Beautiful places, things, environments, sights, sounds and experiences all foster a reverence for reality.

So I do all I can to add touches of beauty to my classes. I dress as attractively as I can. I often bring flowers or art works. I make use of candles. At times I rearrange the whole classroom to create a different environment. I often play beautiful music keyed to the central theme and feelings of the lesson.

Reverence and Prayer

The more reverent our children become, the more their gift of humanness is developed. The more their humanness is developed, the more their spirits are enhanced, which brings us to the act of praying, an expression and an attitude of the Spirit.

Most children, when invited to pray, will become still. Their personal and inner connectedness with God somehow takes over. In prayer most children are innately reverent, unless the prayer is too long and laborious. This rich resource in children should be exploited, in the best sense of the word, which means that while they are children they should be involved in countless prayer experiences—prayer in which they simply are present to God in silence, prayer in which they keep their hands folded or uplift them in a gesture of adoration, prayer in which they kneel in a gesture of humility, prayer in which they prostrate themselves or beat their breasts in a gesture of sorrow, prayer in which they use their bodies to reveal to God the reverence they have for him, prayer in which they use words.

A reverent child is a child who will be open to mystery and in awe of it. This attitude is the cornerstone of faith in a God who cannot be seen or touched. It is essential for prayer.

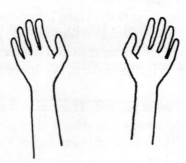

Things to Think About

1. How respectful and reverent a person do you feel you are in relation to yourself, other people, things and God?

2. What do you think causes many children to become more disrespectful and/or less reverent as they grow?

3. What ways have you found effective in helping children become more respectful and reverent?

Things to Do

1. Find a few quiet moments and examine your strengths and weaknesses as a teacher in fostering respect and reverence in your students. Then decide on one specific way you will improve your skills at fostering reverence in each of these four areas: respect for self, for others, for things, for God. Evaluate your progress at the end of each class for about a month.

2. As a help to yourself and your students in discovering how present or absent is reverence in contemporary society, go through several magazines and/or newspapers. Tear out any pictures, ads, headlines, stories that reveal reverence—for self, for others, for things—and also any such items that reveal a lack of reverence or respect for self, people, things. Study the two sets of findings and draw your conclusions. Perhaps create a display or a report to share what you found.

3. Make a list of people you feel manifest a strong sense of respect or reverence for themselves, other people and things. Reflect on how you could become more like them in aspects of respect or reverence you feel weakest in.

11
Stillness

One of the briefest of the psalms pictures the faith-filled person as a quiet child with its mother.

> I have stilled and quieted
>   my soul like a weaned child.
> Like a weaned child on its mother's lap (131:2).

How often have we delighted at the sight of a child resting quietly on its mother's lap as she holds her baby tenderly but securely! A child in that moment is the perfect image of one who is wholly still inside and out because she or he is totally content and secure in the embrace of a loving mother. It is the perfect picture of a prayerful person.

Other images of that same child may quickly jar the comforting silence. Often such quiet moments, even in the life of a well cared for infant, seem the exception.

We and our children live in a world increasingly polluted by noise. Richard Reichert, a highly respected religious educator, father of several growing children, expressed his belief that by the time children today become teenagers they are addicted to noise. From experience and observation many parents and teachers share his belief.

The noises of life do not themselves destroy faith and inhibit prayer. After all, the central revelation of God to the Jews occurred at Mount Sinai amidst awesome rumbling thunder and crackling lightning bolts (Ex 19:16-19). And Jesus communed prayerfully with his father in busy village marketplaces, amidst the shouting and shoving of shoppers and merchants. Prayer is possible on a noisy city street or crowded, screeching subway. A prayerful person can pray even amidst the deafening amplified sound of a rock concert. It is important that we teach our children to find God in the normal contexts of life, which tend more and more to be polluted with noise.

But centuries of experience within all religious traditions teach the importance of outer silence and inner stillness for a life of prayer. The *National Catechetical Directory* draws on that wisdom in affirming: "In seeking intimacy with God, silence is necessary; for prayer is a conversation, in which one must listen as well as speak" (#143).

The prophet Elijah, when he climbed the same mountain of Sinai, experienced God's presence not in thunder, lightning, deafening winds and earthquake, but in "a tiny whispering sound" (1 Kgs 19:12), "the murmur of a gentle breeze." And Jesus often stole off from the noise of the marketplace to the quiet of the seaside, desert, mountains, and gardens to commune in silent stillness with his Father (Lk 5:16; Mk 1:35; Lk 6:12; Lk 22:29).

His example of withdrawing from the daily noises of city life became institutionalized in the lives of the early cenobites and monks and later in the monastic orders and religious communities. For those Christians remaining engaged in secular life, Jesus' temporary periods in quiet, isolated places have been imitated in the tradition of days of recollection, retreats and daily times for undisturbed meditation.

One psalm verse captures the thrust of this tradition of silence as a vital condition for learning to commune with God: "Be still, and know that I am God" (Ps 46:10). As catechists we have the privilege and challenge of helping our students learn to find outer and inner silence for prayer, which in turn will enable them to find ways to pray even in the active, noise-saturated world in which they seem so much at home.

Learning to Be Still

I find that children of any age respond quickly and well to an invitation to stillness and silence. It seems that the human spirit hungers for a periodic cessation of noise and activity. Perhaps, because the human spirit is so young and fresh in children, it desperately needs stillness and silence to grow. Perhaps, too, children respond so well to the invitation to become still and quiet because it is as much a need as food, shelter and clothing, but is rarely met in their lives.

I have found that even the most difficult groups of children often respond positively to an invitation to become still. For example, several years ago I was teaching religion to 14 sixth graders in a once-a-week situation. From the first class they responded disdainfully to things that were part of the teaching-learning situation and were almost abusive toward the content, toward me and toward one another. Some nights after class I cried in anguish about the way they were.

A turning point in the situation came quite unexpectedly midway through the year. I prepared a guided meditation to begin that particular class but I didn't announce that we were going to meditate. I simply began the class by inviting them to become still and I guided them in doing so. "Place your feet flat on the floor, lay your hands quietly in your lap, close your eyes and breathe quietly—so quietly that you can hear your breathing."

When they were completely still, I took them on a guided journey with Jesus using a story from the New Testament. To my great surprise all of them did it. And a marked change of attitude flowed out of the prayer into the remainder of the class.

But what surprised me most was Tim's question at the beginning of the next class: "Are we going to meditate again today?"

Silence and stillness are the most available prayer tools there are. They are also, I feel,

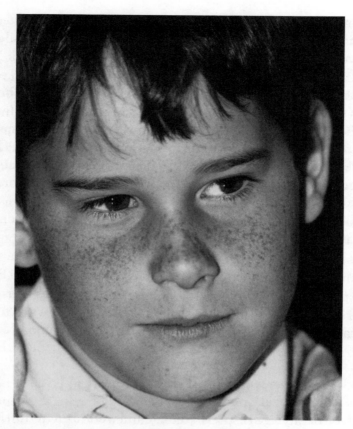

among the most effective. Students can be invited into silence and helped to become to-tally still, so that they can listen to and hear what is going on within themselves. They can be helped to become aware that what God has to say to them has more of a chance of being heard if they make silent spaces for hearing and listening.

Besides guided meditations there are other ways to pray in silence and stillness with children.

For example, when I am preparing my lessons I am alert to times when a pause for stillness and silence might be appropriate. It might be following the reading of a Bible story. It might be between phrases of spoken prayer. It might be near the end of class as a movement in the culminating activities. It might be built into the breaks between learn-ing about their lives, learning about their faith and learning how to live their faith. Or, no matter what the plan, moments of silence might happen unpredictably as the Spirit sug-gests in the course of the class itself.

Sometimes prayerful silence occurs following the placing of a question and the forth-coming of an answer. The burden of this kind of silence being productive falls upon the teacher. If he or she is discomforted when children don't respond quickly, and habitually fills up the pause with qualifying or explanatory words, this kind of silence will rarely happen.

In each of my classes I create an opportunity for this kind of silence by indicating to the children that I'm going to ask a question that each one may have a different answer for. I pause momentarily. Then I tell them that once I have placed the question we will all think in silence about it for a few moments. I pause again momentarily. Then I solemnly place the question and we wait in silence together as we reflect interiorly about possible and individual answers. Sometimes I tell them that I feel the Spirit was working overtime, especially if the answers are honest, thoughtful and insightful.

Another thing that I do is what I have named "silent reverie." Following a brief explanation about a doctrinal teaching I will invite the children to take a few moments to "talk to themselves" about the belief that is suggested. I give them time, in silence, to talk to themselves. After the time of silence, I ask each one to share one thing that he or she has said to himself or herself. Then I may repeat what most of them said to themselves and suggest that as they talk to themselves during the day, they might add that to their conversations with themselves.

Besides individual techniques of fostering moments of silence while learning and praying in class, I believe that one of the most important things I as a teacher can do to help children learn inner and outer stillness is to create an orderly, peaceable classroom environment.

Often children come to religion class not just from a noisy world, but carrying with them an inner din that is even louder. Inner noise involves feelings of stress, inadequacy, anger, frustration, ambition, confusion, worries, despair. Such internal noises make it impossible to hear God's gentle voice and respond to it. Without feeling that one needs to be a therapist or counselor a teacher can do much to still the inner turmoil that drowns out any meaningful prayer.

To be a kind of gentle presence that many children experience nowhere else takes practice and can often be a challenge. Some rules: Speak calmly and quietly. Never yell. Work out four or five firm rules of classroom conduct with the children that are agreed upon as necessary and inviolable. Insist on mutual respect and listening. Involve the children in activities that engage and challenge them. Insist on silence while the students are reading or doing individual work.

These simple but important techniques of classroom management make it possible for children to experience a general sense of inner and outer quiet, order and peace. In such a climate moments of prayerful silence become possible and meaningful.

The more I foster silence in my religion classes, the more I realize how nurturing it is and the more ideas I get about ways and times for building silence into the instructions.

Finally, I have a suspicion that because children feel that the invitation to be silent and still is a time to "do nothing" (something they enjoy doing), they are unusually responsive to the invitation. All that happens in these "do nothing" moments often comes as a surprise to them, which increases their desire and willingness to do more of it.

What a blessed tool is silence, stillness. To use it often and well is to give the Holy Spirit an equal partnership in the act of helping our children grow in faith and in love of Yahweh.

Things to Think About

1. How do you feel about silence, about inner and outer stillness? How able are you to tolerate silence? How much do you fear it or find it makes you tense and uncomfortable? Why?

2. What do you find most helps you become silent within? How important to you is outer silence for achieving inner stillness?

3. What keeps your life filled with noise, inside and out? What effects of this noise pollution do you see in your life?

Things to Do

1. Set aside for yourself a regular period of silence each day. Begin with a short time, even five minutes. Sit quietly and let your whole body relax. Breathe slowly, deeply. As you become more quiet, imagine a beautiful scene in which you find peace and stillness, or read several verses of scripture, or pray in any way that is comfortable, or let your mind find its own focus, or use pencil, crayons or paints and write or draw quietly. Mostly just enjoy the stillness. Gradually increase the time and explore various approaches to silence and prayer.

2. In planning your lessons deliberately look for ways of building moments and periods of silence into them. Firmly but gently guide the children in developing skills for working and praying silently.

3. Memorize the verse "Be still, and know that I am God" (Ps 46:10). Pray it from time to time during the day as a reminder of God's call to build more silence into your life as a help to coming to know God better.

12
Compassion and Justice

My dad was a remarkable man. He was an Iowa farmer who knew good times and bad times. Most of the time he loved to celebrate life and its joys. Sometimes he found it hard to cope and eased life's burdens with alcohol, until one Lent he gave up drinking for good.

In his own way he was a very prayerful man. We drove eight miles to church every Sunday no matter what the weather or the condition of the dirt and gravel roads. We prayed the Rosary as a family every evening, all year. He thanked God for good weather and good harvests and for his family. He was quick to ask God's forgiveness. He asked God for sun and rain, for money enough to feed us all. He loved to celebrate the church's feasts and holidays.

But what I remember most is how sensitive and compassionate he was. Without any training he knew how to heal ailing animals, so much so that neighboring farmers called on Dad at all hours to help them with a sick cow or horse. And anyone's bad luck or pain could empty his pockets. He was always giving his time, his limited cash, whatever anyone needed. He could never say no to someone who was hurting and asked for help.

His spirit of compassion and generosity was contagious, even though I remember times my mom and some of us children were angry at Dad for giving away something we felt we needed.

As a child I never linked Dad's prayerfulness with his willingness to reach out to anyone in pain or need. But now I see how connected are compassion and prayer. I've come to believe that without a compassionate spirit it's not possible to pray very well.

Hebrew Prophets

The ancient Hebrew prophets went out of their way to make just that point.
Amos has God expressing hatred for the people's prayers because of their lack of com-

passion and justice, concluding that "if you would offer me holocausts, / then let justice surge like water, / and goodness like an unfailing stream" (Am 5:21-24).

Isaiah says God refuses to hear or respond to the prayers and fasts of the people because they seek only their own pleasure and oppress their workers. It is not enough to bow one's head, and lie in sackcloth and ashes before the Lord.

> This, rather, is the fasting that I wish:
>   releasing those bound unjustly,
>   untying the thongs of the yoke;
> Setting free the oppressed,
>   breaking every yoke;
> Sharing your bread with the hungry,
>   sheltering the oppressed and the homeless;
> Clothing the naked when you see them,
>   and not turning your back on your own (Is 58:6-7).

Isaiah concludes with God's promise that if the people begin acting with that kind of compassion and justice, then God will hear their prayers and respond to their fasts.

Jeremiah is just as clear on this point, going so far as to say that unless one acts with compassionate justice, he or she simply does not know God:

> [Your father] did what was right and just,
>   and it went well with him.
> Because he dispensed justice to the weak and the poor,
>   it went well with him.
> Is this not true knowledge of me?
>   says the LORD (Jer 22:15-16).

Jesus Christ

Jesus echoes these prophets of old. In fact his whole life is a parable of the prophetic teaching. The gospels reveal him intentionally taking his place with the poor and needy—lepers, prostitutes, tax collectors, foreigners—reaching out in God's name to those whom the religious orthodoxy of his time considers outside God's law. Jesus' life is a prophetic challenge to those who see religion as primarily the correct performance of ritual prayers and sacrifices.

Jesus teaches that if you are not in harmony with your brother or sister, you can't be in harmony with God: "Therefore, if you bring your gift to the altar, and there recall that your brother has anything against you, leave your gift there at the altar, go first to be reconciled with your brother, and then come and offer your gift" (Mt 5:23-24).

Two of Jesus' most famous stories or parables make it very clear that compassion is an absolute condition for true prayer and ultimately for salvation.

The story of the Good Samaritan is evidently about being compassionate. But the story notes that it is a Samaritan, one outside God's law and God's people, whose heart is touched by the robbers' victim. The two who pass by the bleeding man are a Jewish priest and his assistant, a Levite, who hurry by on their way to the Temple. Compassion is, for Jesus, the condition for true temple worship, and indeed, for inheriting everlasting life (Lk 10:25-37).

When, near the end of his life, Jesus speaks of the final judgment, he makes it clear that compassion and justice are the criteria for passing. "For I was hungry and you gave me food, I was thirsty and you gave me drink, a stranger and you welcomed me, naked and you clothed me, ill and you cared for me, in prison and you visited me." When the just express wonder at when they did this for him, Jesus concludes with the awesome assertion that "whatever you did for one of these least brothers of mine, you did for *me*" (Mt 25:31-46).

A Prophetic Church

Jesus' disciples did not forget Jesus' point even though many of them had considerable difficulty living lives of justice and compassion. Early Christian writings repeatedly call those who claim to follow Jesus to examine how justly and compassionately they are living, as well as how faithfully they pray.

James put it this way: "Religion that is pure and undefiled before God and the Father is this: to care for orphans and widows in their affliction . . ." (Jas 1:27). He proceeds to spell this out very concretely in terms of the Christian communities to whom he wrote. "If a brother or sister has nothing to wear and has no food for the day, and one of you says to them, 'Go in peace, keep warm and eat well,' but you do not give them the necessities of the body, what good is it? So also faith of itself, if it does not have works, is dead" (Jas 2:14-17).

Paul sums up the law of Christ is these words: "Bear one another's burdens" (Gal 6:2).

And John asks, "If someone who has worldly means sees a brother in need and refuses him compassion, how can the love of God remain in him?" (1 Jn 3:17). He answers his own question in the strongest terms: "Whoever does not love a brother whom he has seen cannot love God whom he has not seen. This is the commandment we have from him: whoever loves God must also love his brother" (1 Jn 4:20-21).

The same conviction permeates the writings of Christians after New Testament times. Tertullian stresses that a "procession of good works" should accompany our prayer on its path to the altar. Cyprian and others call prayer that is not accompanied by almsgiving a "barren prayer."

John Chrysostom is particularly eloquent.

> Do you really wish to pay homage to Christ's body? Then do not neglect him when he is naked. At the same time that you honor him here [in church] with hangings made of silk, do not ignore him outside when he perishes from cold and nakedness. For the One who said, 'This is my body'. . . . also said 'When I was hungry you gave me nothing to eat.' . . . Your brother is more truly his temple than any church building.

From the early church down to our own times, at its best moments, and in its best individuals and communities, Christianity has exemplified this intimate connection between devotion and compassion. Along with glorious cathedrals for prayer medieval Christians created hospitals and soup kitchens and a wealth of social services. Saints admired for their prayerful union with God were equally admired for their selfless dedication to the poor and sick—St. Frances of Rome, St. Martin of Tours, St. Francis of Assisi, St. Elizabeth of Portugal.

And in our own times it is striking that perhaps the four most widely admired modern Catholics—Mother Teresa, Thomas Merton, Dorothy Day and Pope John Paul II—are prayerful persons whose contemplative lives are intertwined with a tireless concern for the victims of poverty, hunger, homelessness, war and injustice.

The popes of the last hundred years, and our American bishops with them, have consistently and ever more urgently linked compassion and justice with union with God.

And the Children?

It is important that our catechesis of children reflect this intimate link between compassion and justice and prayer—without placing burdens on them beyond their young years or causing needless guilt.

I try to pray with the children in every class. I also try in my classes to open them to the sufferings of real people in the world around them. Sometimes the hurting people are close indeed—at home, among their families.

Field Trips, Service Projects

In our parish the children, from the earliest grades on, have opportunities for contact with the poor. One class each week visits a local soup kitchen. At home the families of children prepare large batches of chili, using a recipe the soup kitchen provided. Then on Sunday morning the children, with their families, take their meal to the soup kitchen, and, depending on the age of the children, assist in feeding the homeless and hungry who come for food.

Older children, especially those preparing for confirmation, become involved in a variety of other service projects that bring them into direct contact with the sick, the aged, the poor and the needy in our city. Such projects need to be very carefully planned beforehand, supervised during, and then discussed afterwards.

Prayers

A prayer we pray often is Francis' Peace Prayer ("Lord, make me an instrument of your peace . . . "). It seems to sum up as well as any single prayer the relation between prayer and compassion, justice and peace. It is a prayer worth having the children memorize. I often give them small, attractive cards with the Peace Prayer printed on it. The prayer has been put to music by several musicians. Carl and I like to play a recording of the song-prayer as the children work quietly at a project.

Another way of helping the children grow in compassion as they become more prayerful is to have them write brief prayers modeled on the general intercessions prayed at Mass. We ask the children to think of people who are hurting and in need. It often works best if they write out their petitions. Then we gather our prayers together just as at Mass, concluding each petition with a common prayer, like "Lord, hear our prayer."

Sometimes we have found it useful to have the children build their prayer petitions from pictures they have been using—media photos or art works of the poor, lonely, sick, homeless, unemployed and addicts.

Sometimes, too, we will simply hang such photos or art works around the room as part of the environment. The youngsters may gaze at one or another of the pictures from time to time. We also introduce one or more of the visuals at an appropriate moment in the development of our lesson. It is important that our children grow up with an increasing awareness of how people in our cities, on our farms, in our world are suffering.

Simulation Games

We also at times share with them stories from the daily paper, stories of local people in real need. Sometimes, too, we engage them in simulation games that allow them to *feel* the injustices that are part of so many people's lives. For example, with a group of eighth graders, a year or two ago, we gave them some "M & M's" for a snack. We had prepared small paper plates with varying numbers of candies on each—accurately reflecting world food distribution statistics. Most had just one "M & M." A few had two, less had three, and one plate had 43! It was interesting how the youngsters reacted as they discovered how unjustly we were distributing their snack. Lauren, who received the largest number, began to feel the hurt and anger of his classmates. He quickly told them, "I don't like green ones. I'll give you all my green ones!"

Afterwards we reflected with them on the actual statistics of food distribution around the world—facts that tended to be *felt* now from their personal reactions to the unjust snack. It is important that the youngsters become more aware as they get older of the social, economic and political dimension of injustice and suffering. Christian compassion for individual sufferers needs to expand to an awareness of unjust institutions, systems and structures that *cause* hurts to millions of people. Christians are called to transform those societal sources of suffering as well as to reach out to suffering individuals.

Books, Films, Videos, Slides

We've also used some excellent movies and videos with different grade levels and superb children's books. Two books that speak to younger children are *Natural History* by M.B. Goffstein and *Tico and the Golden Wings* by Leo Lionni, and with older children, Marcia Brown's *Stone Soup, Trevor's Place* by Frank and Janet Terrell, and *The Story of Jumping Mouse* by John Steptoe. There are many more. (See the Bibliography at the back of this book.)

Two films we've found particularly moving in terms of compassion are both based on stories by Tolstoy: *A Christmas Gift* and *Martin the Cobbler* (Billy Budd Films). These stories easily lend themselves to further exploration of the call to compassion and justice and to prayer.

Slides, too, can be very useful. With a junior high class we showed slides of impoverished children in Honduras. We had been there the preceding year and had taken many pictures. The sight of malnourished children, of children their age "guarding" cars to make money for their families, begging us for pencils and paper—most of the children cannot go to school—touched the youngsters. We then looked at a slide of a Nicaraguan peasant's painting of Jesus' story of the Good Samaritan, taken from *The Gospel in Art by the Peasants of Solentiname* (see Bibliography). We talked about the story in the light of the photos we had just been viewing.

Then we showed some slides of four Vietnam veterans who were fasting, about a mile from our classroom, on the U.S. Capitol steps in protest against aid to the Contras. We considered whether these four fasters were following out Jesus' call in the Good Samaritan story. We discussed how effective their fasting might be or not be in helping the poor of Central America, people like the children whose pictures we had been looking at.

We then gave those students who wished to do so the opportunity to write the four fasting veterans brief letters. Most of the letters expressed admiration for their courage and commitment but criticized their strategy of fasting. Finally we created a litany of prayers for the poor children and for the four fasters. It was a fascinating class in which the youngsters expanded their awareness of human suffering and injustice and looked at one way four serious Christians were following up Jesus' call to compassion and justice.

Sunday Eucharist

Our parish closely relates compassion and justice with Sunday worship. One of the most exciting Sunday Masses each year is Toy Sunday during Advent. The children of the whole parish bring good toys they are willing to share with poor children in an inner-city parish. They bring up their toys and place them all around the altar at the end of the Liturgy of the Word. It is a sight to behold, mountains of toys almost engulfing the altar.

Periodically during the year there are food collections for the poor at the Sunday Masses.

A simple but important practice that our godchildren have done from their earliest days is to hand in their family's contribution at collection time. For them it is a kind of high point of participation in the Sunday Eucharist. They know that coming to church to pray includes bringing money for the needs of the parish community and the world beyond its boundaries.

In a world in which many of the children we teach have much more than they need and often tend not to appreciate the good things with which they have been blessed, I feel we catechists have a privileged position. We can help them open their eyes and hearts to the millions who have little or none of what they have. We can expand their consciousness to the pain and hurt all around them, and provide them with examples of compassionate, just Christians, and with opportunities to reach out to help in small but meaningful ways. My dad did that for me.

Things to Think About

1. What is more important to you in your Catholic life, prayer or works of compassion and justice?

2. Why do the Jewish and Christian traditions stress compassion and justice as conditions for sincere prayer?

3. Who are some people who attract you or challenge you by their prayerful and compassionate lives?

Things to Do

1. In your bible look up the texts cited above. Read them there in their broader context. For example, read the entire chapter in the Bible in which a given text appears. If you have time, read the whole book, for example, the entire prophecy of Amos, Micah, Isaiah or Jeremiah, or the letters of James, John, Peter and Paul. In this way you may get a stronger sense of how closely the Jewish and Christian scriptures relate prayer with acts of compassion and justice.

2. It is said that people today learn 83 percent of what they learn through their eyes, through visuals. Begin a collection of photos and art works that show people hurting, and people helping those who are suffering. Newspapers and magazines of all kinds are good sources of such visuals. Photo and art books can also be great sources. So are museums and even libraries. Display these at appropriate times and use them in your lessons to help nurture compassion in your students.

3. Plan to do something on a monthly basis that is compassionate. It might be writing a letter to someone who loves you but rarely sees or hears from you. It might be visiting a next door neighbor who is unable to get out much. It might be contributing time to a soup kitchen. It might be selecting clothes from your wardrobe and taking them to a distribution center for the needy.

13
Prayerful People

Children subconsciously assimilate what they see the adults in their lives doing. They are great at patterning. Our children reflect their parents, teachers, coaches and other significant adults.

The children who see the important adults in their lives praying will, more often than not, own praying as part of their own lives, both as children and as adults.

Prayerful Parents

Carl often tells a story of a time when he was critically ill with pneumonia as a very young child. Their family doctor told his parents that, if he made it through the night, he would probably live. Carl doesn't remember the illness as much as he remembers his father kneeling for a long time during the night at his bedside praying and begging God to help him live.

I worked for a year with Father Alan Smith, a Dominican priest, and whenever he talked about what had influenced his belief in prayer, actually what had contributed to his decision to become a priest, it was the memory of his father whom he had often seen praying.

When I think of the threads of things that have been sewn inside me by my parents, the most permanent is prayer. They never ate anything, particularly a meal, without asking God to bless it and thanking God for the gift of food. We were reprimanded when we, all too often, started to eat before "grace" was prayed.

Our family prayed the Rosary, not just during the months of May and October, but every night of the year. In my memory, not so happy, is a picture of my family kneeling up against our dining room chairs praying the Rosary with either my dad or mother leading us. On occasions when I feigned illness or weariness right before rosary time in an attempt to escape, my father prayed loudly enough so I could hear him in my upstairs bedroom. He knew that would make me feel guilty. I would, without fail, get up and pray the Rosary. As soon as I rejoined the family at prayer, my father prayed in a normal tone of voice. I laugh about that now, but I learned a lot about praying from my parents' steadfast adherence to it in good times and bad, in sickness and health.

William and Leyda Barbieri, the parents of Angela and Miguel, our godchildren, have made a habit of praying with them before they go to sleep. When Angela travels or spends the night with us, she asks Carl or me to pray with her at bedtime. She has learned to place herself, her family and her friends safely in God's hands while she sleeps. Her parents, prayerful people, have taught her that.

I find, too, that generally children who live with parents who pray have a friendlier attitude toward religion. They come to class with a built-in acquaintance with God and a knowledge that there is a value to learning about their faith.

Parents and religion teachers sometimes need to be reminded of the importance of prayerful people in the everyday lives of their children. It is not enough for children only to see people praying during the liturgy of the Eucharist and other liturgical celebrations, although these times are very important as well.

It would be wise, I think, for parishes to build into their ongoing adult education programs sessions on the importance and need for prayer in the home.

Many books deal very well with this activity in the home, giving many practical hints for praying as a family. See the bibliography at the end of the book for some suggestions.

It takes time and commitment for a family to build a habit of prayer. But it is one of the most important things a family might do if it desires prayerful and faithful children.

Prayerful Catechists

Most people who pray have been influenced by a prayerful person in their childhood and growing up years. Most often, as in the examples above, it is someone with whom they live, parents or grandparents. But for some the influential prayerful person may well be one of their teachers. Catechists often touch children by their prayerful example in class in a way that has lifelong consequences.

One of the major tasks of a catechist is to help children learn to pray. Some catechists see this as a charge to see that their students know the traditional Catholic prayers. Surely this is an important part of helping children become prayerful Catholics. But teaching prayers is not enough.

Children can be taught words of prayers, they can be told how important it is to pray and they can learn many different ways to pray, but on their journey to become pray-ers they need to walk with people who pray.

I remember once teaching a group of fourth graders in a parish religious education program. I asked Carl to come along to observe and critique my teaching. Naturally I built in a number of opportunities for prayer as I always do. To my surprise Carl's criticism focused on those prayer moments. He complimented me on my care to have meaningful forms of prayer several times during the class. But less positively, he pointed out that I seemed so preoccupied with the children—being sure they were praying the right words in the right way—that I was not praying. It was true. And if Carl noticed it, surely the children did, too.

Children notice when we fail to pray when we should. A number of years ago I went regularly to the army base at Fort Belvoir, Virginia, to teach religion on Sundays. Before one of the classes a third grader, with great concern and worry, informed me that her older brother had been missing since Friday. I expressed surprise and tried to console her with some words of hope. She listened and waited for me to do something more. When I didn't she sadly asked me, "Aren't you even going to pray for him?" It was one of the most sobering moments of my long teaching career. It was also a teachable moment because since then I have never failed to suggest prayer when a child confides a concern or worry.

It is as important for religion teachers to pray with their students during each class as it is to introduce them to and teach them other aspects of their tradition and faith.

Children who regularly spend time with a teacher who prays may well associate praying with all that it means to be a faithful believer. A praying teacher is a critical audio-visual in educating children in the importance and value of prayer in a Christian's life. It is doubly helpful when the children see their catechist taking part prayerfully in the Eucharist on Sundays in their parish.

Other Prayerful People

Catechists can also on occasion invite parents or other lay people, a priest, a religious brother, a nun, to pray with them and to answer questions like: Why do you pray? How do you pray? Did you pray as a child? What are your favorite prayers?

Another way to bring your students into contact with prayerful people is through the media. You might share with them all or part of the life story of a saint or other person of great faith and love, or show them a film or video of such a prayerful person as a moving example of the place of prayer in that person's life. Sometimes strong photos of praying people around the world, whether Christian or of other religious traditions, appear in newspapers or magazines. Display one or more of these photos from time to time; then at an appropriate time talk with the students about these prayerful people, or have the children do creative or research activities in relation to the pictured people.

Both parents and teachers, as well as others in the children's faith communities, have a responsibility to model what we hope they will be: prayerful people who will give to future generations the gift of prayer.

Things to Think About

1. Take a few quiet moments to reflect on your own formation in prayer. Who do you remember who struck you as a genuinely prayerful person? What effect on you did such persons have? Who most influenced you to want to become a more prayerful person?

2. Reflect on your religion classes and other contacts with your students. What might let them discover that prayer is an important part of your life? When and where do they actually see you praying? How honestly do you pray in class as you lead the students in prayer?

3. How can you become for the students a more meaningful example of a praying person?

Things to Do

1. Invite a friend or someone else whose judgment you trust to sit in on or to participate in one or more of your classes. Ask for their honest critique. If they do not mention anything about prayer in the class, bring up the subject and ask them about it, and particularly about your own example as a prayerful person.

2. Begin a file—whether an empty drawer, box or actual file—of photos, news reports, stories, even cartoons, about prayerful people. Whenever you see anything about people praying, just clip it out and put it in your file for future use. If you personally experience a noteworthy example of someone praying, write up a brief description of the experience or a story about the person praying. Add it to your file. Then when you need an example of a prayerful person for one of your lessons, go to the file and look for something appropriate.

3. Explore the possibility of joining or beginning a prayer group of a few friends or parishioners. If you are hesitant to organize such a group on your own, talk with your DRE or with your parish priest or other parish minister. Or sound out several friends informally over lunch or coffee. Once you have a small group of four, five or six, you can decide together on how you wish to proceed. The regular contact with others in prayer can be very helpful for some people in their own efforts to grow in a prayerful way of life.

14
Prayerful Times

Anytime is a good time for prayer. "With all prayer and supplication, pray at every opportunity in the Spirit," St. Paul urges us (Eph 6:18).

Praying can be as continuous as breathing. Children can discover that they can pray anytime. An example: While teaching a third grade class, Carl taught the children how to pray the "Jesus Prayer" and prayed it with them. They found it easy and good to pray the name "Jesus" as they breathed in and out. In the succeeding class one of the boys eagerly shared a discovery he had made during the week. "Mr. Pfeifer, do you know what?" "No . . . what, John?" "That Jesus Prayer we prayed last week sitting in a circle on the floor . . . you can pray it when you're walking!"

He had discovered that there is no set time, no particular place in which the "Jesus Prayer" might be prayed. It can be prayed anywhere at any time.

To pray always is the ideal when considering times to pray. But to pray always it helps to have regular, special times for prayer. This has been the experience of all religious traditions. Muslims are called to pray five times each day. Jesus and the Jews of his time prayed three times each day, morning, midday and evening. Christians over the centuries, first in local churches and then in monasteries, developed the Liturgy of the Hours. Once largely restricted to priests, religious and monks, the Liturgy of the Hours is becoming more common in parishes, homes and personal devotions.

Just as certain times in the day are more suitable for prayer, notably morning, evening and meal times, also special times during the week are especially good for prayer, particularly Sunday. Prayer takes on the feeling, color and tone of the special seasons, feasts and holydays during the year that tell anew the story of Jesus' birth, death, resurrection and the sending of his Spirit.

The church has learned from centuries of experience that a rhythm of regular prayer times sustains the spirit eager to pray at all times. Unfortunately, the stresses and rhythms of modern life, especially in families with school-age children, make some of these traditionally special times for prayer difficult to honor—think of the typical morning rush to get ready for work and school! Or evenings with parents working late and children involved in a variety of activities from homework to dance lessons, soccer games and scouting! Individual families need to creatively discover suitable times for prayer in their own circumstances.

The times of prayer during religion classes are also very significant moments. The question of the right time to pray during religion classes often comes up when catechists discuss praying with children.

Almost all teachers in the recent past, and many still today, routinely begin and end religion class, and other classes as well, with a prayer. Often traditional prayers are prayed at these times, for example, the Morning Offering, Our Father, Hail Mary or Glory Be. Some catechists deliberately and carefully continue these practices. Others of us pray at opportune moments during our classes.

We might consider these three times for prayer in our religion classes: at the beginning, at the end, and at moments during the class.

Beginning

If the prayer at the start of class is more an activity to quiet the children than focused praying, it could be a misuse of prayer. On the other hand, if it helps the children become more aware of God's presence with and for them and opens them to the mystery and story of their lives and God's, then it can be the perfect time to pray. Opening prayers can be more effective if they are varied to avoid a deadening routine, if they relate to the topic of the lesson or to some event in the lives of the students, or if they make use of some object, like the Bible, a strong photo or work of sacred art, a moving piece of music.

Ending

With regard to praying at the end of class, there are similar cautions and suggestions. If the closing prayer is primarily a technique for having the children end the class and leave the room in a quiet, orderly fashion, it is less prayer than a form of classroom management. If the closing prayer happens after the scheduled class time is up, or is squeezed into the final moments in a hurried fashion, the children's minds and attention will hardly be on the prayer, but on getting out and on their way. And if the manner of praying at the end of class is predictably routine, the children will find it hard to pray sincerely from the heart.

On the other hand, if the movement of the class culminates in prayer and fits well into the allotted class time, this can be a perfect moment for prayer. It can draw threads of the class and the children together in a prayer that connects their class experience with the rest of their daily lives. Timing is very critical for making a closing prayer experience meaningful. It may not be too rushed, nor too long, nor so short that it remains superficial. Many of the prayer supports suggested above for the opening class prayer are just as useful at the end of class.

During

I tend to prefer giving more attention to moments of prayer during class. Such moments are less predictable for the students and therefore less likely to be superficially routine. They also are experienced as more directly related to and flowing from the learning taking place.

Several potential hazards can be avoided by careful planning and a flexible approach during class. It is important to remain open to the movement of the Holy Spirit within the rhythm of the class as it unfolds, while having specific moments in mind. The great risk here is that an activity takes more time than planned, and as a result the moment planned for prayer is swallowed up. Or, the class develops in an unexpected way and the planned prayer becomes an unrelated add-on, maybe even an intrusion.

On the other hand, if the planning of the class and the way it actually works out makes it possible for the praying to flow out of what is happening, those are perfect prayer times.

To do this kind of praying successfully means mastering the art of timing. Learn how to discern more than one possible praying time while planning the lessons, and how to feel the prayable moment during the actual lesson. If the choice is for praying during class, times of silent prayer as well as verbal prayer will be suitable, and more prayer can happen.

Perhaps an example will suggest the need for planning and the range of possibilities one can explore. It's a first grade class. I have as my goal to help the children become more aware that God is with them, will always be with them and loves them so much that he seeks them out should they try to hide from him.

I begin the class by asking the children to draw a picture of themselves with someone who loves to be with them or to draw someone they like being with as much as possible because it's fun to be with that person and they love him or her.

After they have drawn their pictures and shared stories about the people they pictured they might take their drawings to our "prayer place" (see next chapter). Each child prays aloud a prayer for the person on his or her picture, or we might pray one prayer together thanking God for these people.

Then we would go back to our places and listen to the story, *The Runaway Bunny* by Margaret Wise Brown. After the story we might be silent for a moment or two pondering the great love the mother of the little bunny had for him.

The next thing we would do is gather around the Bible and read Psalm 139 or an adaption of it, like Elspeth Campbell Murphy's *Where Are You God? Psalm 139 for Children*.

Finally we might draw a companion picture for the one we drew earlier in which we picture God with us because he cares so much for us.

After that Psalm 139 might be prayed, even parts of it learned by heart.

The prayer moments are varied and tied intimately with the lesson's development—individual petitions based on their drawings, silent reflection on the piece of children's literature, listening to and then praying Psalm 139 in relation to the Bible and their second drawings. In this lesson there are several prayer moments because of the content. In some lessons there may be only one or two.

When appropriate to the lesson's theme and development the prayer moments in class may also be related to a liturgical season or feast, important times in the children's lives—like birthdays—or to special moments in the life of the parish or nation.

The important thing to remember is that prayer before, during, or after religion classes is vital to what happens to the children's growth in faith. Special class prayer moments can help the children grow in a rhythm of prayer resonating with the ebb and flow of their daily experiences. They need to be planned carefully ahead of time, but you need to remain open to the Spirit, ready to adapt your plan to prayerful moments as they arise during class. In this way our students can gradually learn to "pray constantly."

Things to Think About

1. What are your best times for prayer—each day, each week, each month, each year? What is it about these times that make them more suitable to you for prayer?

2. How carefully do you plan for moments of prayer in your classes? What steps can you take to make your religion classes more prayerful?

3. How closely do you come to St. Paul's ideal of constant prayer? What keeps you from having more moments of prayer in your days? What can you do to find more fruitful prayer times?

Things to Do

1. Buy or borrow a prayer book that includes or adapts the church's Liturgy of the Hours. Try for a week or two to pray faithfully at least Morning Prayer and Evening Prayer. At the end of the trial period, evaluate your experience, and make further plans for regular prayer times.

2. In planning your next several lessons, give extra attention to times in class for prayer. Be sure the prayer times are varied, creative and flow naturally from what you plan to have happen in the class. After these classes spend some time evaluating the prayer moments. From your successes and failures learn for more effective prayer times in future classes.

3. Determine one or two times a day that you plan to give to prayer. Choose the times you feel are best for you, and adjust their length to what you feel is most realistic. Then try to be faithful to these prayer times during one week. Afterwards evaluate your experience and keep or change the times accordingly. Over a period of a month or two, with these weekly checks, you may discover a whole new rhythm of prayer that works best for you.

15
Prayerful Places

When I was eight or nine, my oldest brother, then 10 or 11, and I were trusted to go to Sunday Mass on our own. We sat in the pew that our family worshipped in every Sunday. One of my dad's uncles was in the pew, also. During the Mass, which was long, I became restless, started whispering to my brother, and did other things like giggle, let the kneeler drop a couple of times, and turn my back to the altar to watch the choir in the gallery. A couple of times my uncle placed his right hand tightly over my left one in an effort to stop me from misbehaving in church. I simply wiggled my hand loose and continued being "wicked."

Before we got to my grandparents' house after Mass, they had been told about how I had acted in church. They were really upset with me and told my parents all about my behavior when they came to pick us up. My parents were mortified and angry. They roundly scolded and grounded me.

One of the worst things a child could do at that time, not only in my family but in many others, was to be irreverent in church. The church, the house of God, was considered such a sacred place that to laugh, talk, create undue noise, turn around or misbehave in any way was totally out of order. To do so was to be irreverent toward God and that was unimaginable. It ranked pretty close to being sacrilegious.

Unfortunately I can hardly ever remember enjoying church as a child, but I do remember and appreciate the sense of reverence for the sacred that was instilled in me.

I learned how to be quiet and still within sacred space. I was taught gestures of reverence such as genuflection, folding hands, bowing the head and ways of keeping the body erect—no slouching allowed.

Today children are given much more freedom in church, still sacred space, and I am happy that this is so. Yet, I feel that many children today risk growing up with a very limited sense of reverence in church and other sacred places. In fact they may never have really experienced the value of sacred space.

Most religious traditions recognize the importance of sacred places. We are familiar with Hindus going to the Ganges River to bathe in its water, with Muslims travelling to worship at Mecca, with Jews visiting Jerusalem and Christians making pilgrimages to the Holy Land. We are aware, too, of other special places sacred to many Catholics: Rome, Lourdes, Fatima, Guadalupe.

We believe that in one sense all space and every place is sacred. The Jewish and Christian scriptures reveal that God is everywhere and may be encountered in the most unexpected places. Psalm 139 is perhaps the most loved biblical expression of this belief in God's "omnipresence." But many other biblical stories suggest God's presence everywhere.

Jacob, for example, lay down to sleep one night on a stone at a place called Luz and experienced God's presence through a dream. "Truly, the Lord is in this spot, although I did not know it!" he cried out in wonder on awaking. "How awesome is this shrine! This is nothing else but an abode of God." He took the stone on which he had rested his head in sleep, set it up as a memorial, poured oil over it and renamed the place Bethel, "house of God" (Gn 28:10-16). Bethel remained a sacred place for the Israelites.

Centuries later Moses encountered God in a flaming bush in the desert and reverently removed his shoes, sensing that he stood on holy ground (Ex 3).

Wandering later through the desert Moses and the liberated Israelites set up amidst their tents the special "tabernacle" or "tent of meeting," the special dwelling place of the Lord with his nomadic people (Ex 33:7-11). It was the place Israel could meet Yahweh through Moses. The "ark of the covenant" was placed in the tabernacle (Ex 25—26). Later, under David and Solomon the Temple in Jerusalem replaced the portable tabernacle as the central meeting place with the Lord (1 Kgs 6).

Jesus and the Jews of his time turned reverently to Jerusalem, especially the Temple, as a place specially graced by the presence of God. The gospels show how Jesus loved to spend time in the Jerusalem Temple, as a child yearly with his family, and much more frequently as an adult. His anger at those who abused the Temple suggests the depth of his reverence for it as "a house of prayer" (Mt 21:12-17).

When not in Jerusalem, Jesus regularly went to the synagogue to pray with the local Jewish community and to teach (Mt 9:35; 12:9-15). In Luke's gospel Jesus announces his mission and ministry in the synagogue at Nazareth, where he had prayed with Mary and Joseph since his childhood (Lk 4).

Ordinary places like Luz and a desert bush become sacred places because of remarkable encounters with God there. Other places, like Jerusalem, the Temple, and the synagogues were designated sacred by the community as special places to worship the ever-present God. This is true of most cathedrals, churches, chapels, temples, shrines, houses of prayer—any place built for people to gather in worship or to sit in silence before God.

Prayerful places are important because they can be oases from noise and busyness. They also provide a context for silent reflection on what's going on inside one's heart and one's life. They are places for community worship, liturgy, as well as for individual prayer. They are also a sign of God's presence within a rural village, a town, a city. Sacred places allow us to become more aware that God is with us in every place.

As catechists we have an opportunity and a responsibility to help our students become familiar with places sacred to Catholics and other believers, understand and appreciate the importance of these sacred places to people and experience the value of sacred places for their own prayer. We can do all this partially in religion class and partially through field trips, guided tours and pilgrimages. Our focus here is more on their experience of sacred space in relation to prayer.

Outside the Classroom

I have found that fewer and fewer of my students have regular experiences of praying in sacred places. The practice of making visits to the local parish church or school chapel is no longer as popular as when I was young. Many children in my classes have limited experience of worship in their parish church simply because their families participate in Sunday Mass only occasionally.

To acquaint the children in our classes with sacred space Carl and I take them on a tour of their parish church. We have found it a worthwhile experience. Before making the "field trip" to the church, we spend some time preparing the children. I sometimes give them a worksheet or checklist to complete as we take our guided tour. Some of the items to include in the checklist would be pews, altar, crucifix, candles, pulpit, bible, statues, baptistry, tabernacle, windows, reconciliation room and other distinctive features. Before going we comment briefly on each aspect of the church, both inside and outside, which they find on their checklist. The same approach may be used for tours of a school chapel.

Then we go to the church. Sometimes children bring cameras as well as their checklists. We start on the outside, then go inside for an overview of the whole interior, and then go around to the key places in the church. We encourage the children to check their lists and make any notes about each section or item. We invite the children to come close to the altar. We let them stand at the ambo and touch the Lectionary or Bible. We kneel at the tabernacle. We go into the reconciliation rooms. We explore the baptistry. We walk along the way of the cross. We look at the stained glass windows and statues. We go into the sacristy. We show them the sacred vessels, bread (hosts) and wine, vestments. Where possible, we invite the parish priest to demonstrate and explain the use of the sacred vessels and vestments.

We insist on a quiet, reverent manner, especially as we allow them such close contact with sacred objects. We also pray at some of the key places.

At the end of the tour, or in the next class, we talk together about what we saw and heard. We run through their checklists and invite the children to share any comments they wrote, any drawings they made or photos they took. We try to get at what most inspired and impressed them.

Where it is possible, we also think it important to take children on occasional field trips and tours of other sacred places within their locality. Especially important is the diocesan cathedral. Other possibilities are any important shrines, even if they have only local significance, or perhaps places sacred to other Christians, to Jews, Muslims and those of other religious traditions. We would follow a process similar to that described for touring the parish church. Always focus on an experience of reverence in a sacred place rather than just information about the place. A pilgrimage exemplifies a prayerful approach to visiting a sacred place.

Within the Classroom

We don't always need a special building to have a prayerful place. In a classroom an area can be identified as a "prayer corner." It can be a place where the children are free to go when they want to pray or to be still for awhile. It can be a place where you and the children go to pray.

It can be a big or a small space. If the classroom is small, the space need only be big enough to have the Bible enthroned or to have an icon or a piece of sacred art or a statue or a religious symbol displayed. A comfortable chair or pillows on the floor are good additions to a prayer corner if the space allows. Sometimes a candle or flowers add a special touch to the prayer place.

I have found that most chldren adapt readily and easily to space set aside for prayer. Many children appreciate it because it is perhaps one place in their world where they can go and not be bothered by anyone or anything. Others are fascinated by it because it suggests mystery, a respite from the ordinary. I like it because it keeps me conscious of God's presence with us.

I believe deeply in this kind of space within a classroom in both the parochial and CCD situations because it enables children to learn about and own the sacred space that exists within themselves as they use the place in the classroom designated as sacred space. Some Catholic schools and parish centers may also have a room set aside for quiet prayer and meditation.

We need to refer often to the inner space in children where we believe God dwells so that they discover and own it.

Before praying with children, I nearly always invite them to become quiet so that they can hear God speaking within them or so that they can speak to God dwelling within them.

Beyond special buildings, or parts of a classroom or home, any space can be sacred. Perhaps it is truer to say that all space is sacred, a place where prayer is possible—a prayerful place. We can commune with God on a playground, in a park, in the woods, in the teeming city. God is with us everywhere and where God is the space is sacred.

Things to Think About

1. What are some places especially sacred to you, places where you feel you have experienced or continue to experience God's presence?

2. What can you do to make the room where you teach a more prayerful place? How could you set up a "prayer corner" in that room? How would you like the children to use it?

3. What do you like or dislike about your parish church as a place for prayer? What about it most helps you pray there? What may be a hindrance to your prayer?

Things to Do

1. Set aside some time to make a visit to your parish or other local church, or to a chapel. Spend the time as prayerfully as you can. Feel free to look around—without disturbing other worshippers—to become better acquainted with parts of the sacred place or objects within it. Relax and open yourself to God's presence. Pray as the Spirit moves you.

2. Experiment with a prayer place in your home or apartment. It may be a room where you feel most peaceful, or a corner where you like to sit, or anywhere you feel has potential as a place for prayer. Consider placing a Bible there, and/or a piece of sacred art, an icon, a poster, banner or plaque or other object that you feel may help you pray. Then for a week or two spend a few moments a day in your personal sacred space.

3. Quietly enter into the center of yourself and discover what your inner space is like. What needs to be dusted off and looked at? Does something need healing? Does something need and want to be developed? Are there promptings of the Spirit that you aren't responding to because you're too busy, too afraid, too out of touch with your inner self?

16
Prayerful Positions

Several years ago Carl and I took his parents to visit the Islamic Center in Washington, DC. We removed our shoes according to custom at the entrance of the beautiful mosque. A friendly Muslim man met us and began guiding us on a tour, explaining the religious significance of every fascinating detail of the building.

Suddenly a loud chant-like cry interrupted our tour. The guide respectfully told us it was a call to prayer. He would have to leave us for a few moments.

We watched him kneel down on both knees, then bow deeply, touching the carpeted floor with his forehead. He remained in that reverent position for a short time. Several times he repeated the identical ritual. Then he returned to us and continued the guided tour.

We were touched by his devout faith. Not knowing the language of his prayer, we could sense his prayerfulness through the reverence of his bodily movements and positions. He prayed with his body as much as with words.

The experience remains a compelling example of the power of prayerful positions. Catholic prayer traditions regard highly the role of bodily position in prayer. Any position can be a prayerful one; the position of the body is very flexible as far as prayer is concerned. Yet Catholic pray-ers over the centuries have found certain positions particularly helpful to praying.

Kneeling

When I was a child, kneeling seemed to be the most perfect position for prayer. We knelt often during Mass and even at home, except for meal and bedtime prayers. No matter that we folded the top of our body comfortably over a chair we were kneeling by, that position was important to the praying that we were doing. It suggested an attitude of reverence. It revealed an attitude of submission to God, of humility before the Lord. It could also be uncomfortable to the knees and back which made it a most desirable position because it was doing something extra for God to whom we owed everything. More than any direction that I remember from my childhood prayerlife, it was "kneel up straight" with a not-so-gentle nudge to help me do it. Only now do I understand those good reasons for kneeling at prayer.

Though not as much, kneeling is still part of our Catholic positioning before God as a prayerful expression of our recognition of God's greatness and our dependence on God. However, if you are aware of the young children in your midst during Mass when the congregation kneels, many of them remain sitting on the pew or the kneeler. Most of the older children kneel but they seem to do so automatically. Therefore, this might be a prayerful position that children could learn about in religion classes—a position that might also be practiced.

While not as appropriate to the religion class as to liturgical worship and individual private prayer, kneeling can on occasion be useful in class as well. The children might kneel while praying an expression of sorrow, or while reflecting prayerfully on the sufferings of Jesus or of a modern martyr.

Standing

Standing is one of the most traditional positions for prayer in the Judaeo-Christian tradition. Catacomb paintings show Christians standing in prayer with their arms held outward and upward. Standing shows respect, attentiveness, readiness. It is also symbolic of the resurrection of Jesus Christ and our share in his rising up from defeat and death. We stand to listen to the gospel. In many parishes Catholics stand during the Eucharistic Prayer. We stand to receive the Eucharist and for the final blessing which sends us forth to live out what we have heard and celebrated.

In religion class standing is almost as meaningful as in the church's liturgy. It is an appropriate position for an opening and closing prayer. It can be a sign of prayerful openness to God's word during the reading of a gospel text, particularly during a planned prayer experience. Standing can be a sign of respect for God's word and readiness to respond to it, especially where the Bible is enthroned and read in the classroom. It is also an appropriate position for a communal prayer, particularly one involving gesture or movement. Aside from its more theological meanings, standing for prayer can be useful in class because most of the class time tends to be spent seated. Just the change to standing can help students pray more alertly.

Sitting

Of all the positions for praying, I prefer sitting with my hands resting on my lap, palms up in a gesture of openness. Sitting in prayer can support a quieting of the whole body which is essential, I believe, for meditative and centering prayer.

In the liturgy we sit during the first and second readings from the Bible, during the homily, and after communion. Sitting is appropriate for reflective listening, for thoughtful meditation, for quiet absorption, for relaxed contemplation.

Most children find sitting quietly and following directions for guided and centering prayer fairly easy to do. Most also like to pray that way. Sometimes I ask them to sit quietly at their usual places, with their feet flat on the floor, their backs straight. At other times we sit together on the floor in a more relaxed position, perhaps with our legs folded.

I have had children ask for that kind of prayer. One thing I have learned is that restlessness occurs if the prayer becomes too drawn out and has too many suggested images and feelings in it. Timing is important; so is simplicity in centering on a single theme expressed in appropriate images.

Lying Down

Lying prostrate (face down) is a liturgical position taken, for example, by those about to be ordained. It is an expression of total submission to God, total need of God. It is probably the position Jesus assumed in his agonized prayer in the olive garden.

Lying down, face down or face up, can be a useful position for private prayer, as long as one does not get so comfortable as to fall asleep. But its use in religion class would probably be quite rare, and would require very careful preparation and management. It might be worth introducing the children to lying down as a legitimate prayer form which they could use when by themselves at home on occasion.

In addition to these more sustained traditional prayer positions there are others that are more temporary or passing. Here are several that may be used in religion class as well as in the liturgy or individual private prayer.

Bowing

Bowing, like kneeling and prostrating, suggests an awareness of our respect for and submission to God. It is the typical Muslim prayer position as we witnessed in the mosque in Washington. Our children need to be instructed in prayerful bowing, for example, as an alternative to genuflecting before the altar or tabernacle, or in prayer before accepting the Bible or Lectionary to read God's word publicly.

Bowing the Head

Bowing the head is another bodily position that is proper to prayer. It is part of the blessing prayer at the end of Mass. The priest or the deacon says, "Bow your heads and pray for God's blessing." By bowing our heads we show that we believe that God will place his hands on each of our heads personally and bless us or that God will extend his hands over all of us in a communal blessing.

Genuflection

Genuflection, a brief kneeling gesture, is a position habitually taken when I was a child before walking into the pew for Mass or other prayertimes in church and when stepping out of the pew to leave the church. This position is one of adoration, of acknowledging Christ's eucharistic presence in the tabernacle. It also was the moment in which you said with your body as well as with your mind and heart that the next moments of your life were given over to your duty to worship and to pray. In leaving the church, it was a gesture of acknowledgment before you turned your back on Christ's eucharistic presence and withdrew.

Today many people still genuflect when they enter and leave churches but just as many do not. This may be because the tabernacle is no longer at the front center of the church, on or behind the altar, and that the priest no longer genuflects as often during the Eucharist as was common in earlier years. I am unsure whether that particular positioning will continue in our Catholic tradition. Perhaps that will depend upon us who are the religion teachers of this and future generations. When I take children on a guided tour of our parish church, I teach them the meaning of the genuflection in the area where the tabernacle is located. We genuflect when we arrive near the tabernacle and before we leave the place.

Other Prayer Postitions

The *hands* can be most expressive of prayer and a major help or hindrance to prayer. I grew up thinking that *folding hands* was the most appropriate thing to do with your hands in prayer. That gesture kept the hands quiet. It also symbolized the raising of heart and mind to God in prayer. This gesture seems less common today, but is one children might become familiar with in their religious education classes.

More common today, perhaps, is *resting hands* quietly on the lap as one prays. Placing the resting hands palms up becomes a gesture of openness and receptivity to God's word.

Upraised hands, with arms held out in front of the body in the manner of the first Christians, can be a meaningful gesture of openness and readiness to whatever God wants.

Holding hands during prayer with others can create a sense of being together in prayer, of belonging to a community of believers, of being accepted by others in the sight of God.

The *eyes* are also important for prayer. Several positions of the eyes can be conducive to prayer. The children have a right to learn these in religion class and get some experience in them there as well.

Perhaps the first that comes to mind is *eyes closed*. Closing the eyes can help avoid outside distractions, allowing for less disturbed prayer. Closed eyes also facilitate focusing on the inner landscape of images and feelings. It is a good positioning of the eyes for meditation and guided imagery prayer.

But *eyes focused* on some object can also be a most prayerful position. Some find it helpful to focus on a burning candle, others on a photo or piece of art, while others focus on

some natural object like a flower or a technological product like a spike or nail (suggesting Jesus' sufferings and death).

And lastly there are the *feet*. Most often for prayer we want to keep our *feet still* to help avoid distractions. But the church in its liturgy, and Christians in their popular devotions, have recognized the value for prayer of *moving feet*, like in processions, or for quiet reflection and prayerful reading. I remember often watching priests walking back and forth praying the breviary. Others find walking to be a most helpful position for prayer, particularly in a quiet place. Many people find walking more relaxing and reflective than kneeling or sitting, particularly if they tend to become drowsy. And for Christians in some cultures processions are a vital expression of community prayer.

Ultimately using our body as well as our minds to pray is admitting that we need to pray with the whole of our selves. Positioning the body prayerfully can support the movement within of the Spirit. As catechists we need to explore and experiment with these various prayer positions, and then guide our students in doing so. The rich variety of bodily positions for prayer allows individuals to find and adopt those that are most helpful to them. See Chapter 25 for further thoughts on praying with bodily gesture and movement.

Normally I prefer to engage the children in one or another bodily position for prayer before explaining it. Once they experience a new prayer position, I draw from them their reactions to it, and then relate their observations to the more traditional theological and spiritual reasons behind that position for prayer.

Things to Think About

1. What is your favorite position for prayer? Why?

2. What positions have you found most and least helpful for prayer?

3. Why do you feel bodily position may be important in helping or hindering prayer?

Things to Do

1. Using the above chapter as a checklist, try in your own prayer the various positions over a period of time. Use one sufficiently long enough to become familiar with it and to be able to assess its impact on your praying. Then try another, perhaps selecting positions to suit the time and place where you pray or other personal factors. It is important to have some experience with these traditional Christian prayer positions to be better able to guide the children.

2. Become familiar with prayer positions from other religious traditions, like Zen, Yoga and Islamic practices. Learn about the position and the reasons for it. Then practice it. If you find it helpful to your own prayer, it might also be something to introduce your students to in relation to more traditional Christian prayer positions.

3. Be more conscious and intentional about the prayer positions that you use during the eucharistic liturgy.

Part 3

What Are Practical Helps to Prayer?

17
Scripture

The most unusual and most valuable year of religious education I experienced in my youth was taught by a priest who told us the very first day that he didn't particularly enjoy teaching religion. He told us that we were not going to use the catechism, which back then was *the* textbook for religion classes.

He asked us all to get bibles for use both in class and at home. Each day he would assign one or more psalms for us to memorize. Classes consisted of learning something about a psalm's meaning, memorizing the psalm and then reciting it aloud.

It wasn't very exciting at the time, but, curiously, I still remember many of the psalm verses I learned by heart in that class decades ago. In times of difficulty, hurt, pain or loss I find that an appropriate verse from a psalm rises up in my consciousness. The same thing happens in times of special joy, celebration, success or satisfaction; in times of need or thanksgiving.

From that priest who was, at the time, unorthodox in the way he taught religion I learned and experienced the richness of the Bible for prayer. Partially because of him I have the Bible enthroned in our home and wherever I go, the Bible goes with me. This is especially true when I go out to teach. I'd like to share with you some of the ways I try to pass on that gift of biblical praying to my students.

Psalm Banking

I have developed a practice I call "Psalm Banking." Just as we put money in the bank, to draw out later when it is needed, I encourage my students to put in their memory banks prayer-verses from the psalms or other biblical prayers for use when needed. I do this "prayer banking" with all my students, no matter what their age.

In nearly every class I involve the students in memorizing a verse of a psalm or other biblical prayer. Most often the verse is taken right from the textbook we are using for the lesson. Or I'll select an appropriate prayer-verse from the Bible, most often from the psalms. Once the students have learned it by heart, we pray it together.

Sometimes the students do something creative with a verse, like making a plaque, sign, poster, banner, pin, or painted rock, with the words of the prayer-verse on it. They are encouraged to place it in their room at home as a reminder and help to pray.

My hope is that they will take these biblical prayers with them into their lives much as I took the psalms I learned so long ago into my life.

Enthroning the Bible

Both for myself and for the students I place the Bible somewhere in the classroom where it is clearly visible—as much in the center of our grouping as possible. A name for placing the Bible in a special place is called "Enthroning the Bible." Depending on circumstances I do my best to make this place as attractive as I can. I try to find a beautiful cloth and small pillow, or stand, on which to place the Bible. I may place one or more candles beside it. I sometimes also place a flower near it. At other times I place a piece of sacred art, a photo, or other symbol, in the same area to help relate the Bible message to the life experience central to the lesson.

We usually gather near the Bible at least once during the class to read and pray from it. Here is an example of how I guided a sixth-grade class to experience the Bible in prayer during a lesson on "The Bible: Our Story."

I placed the Bible on a richly colored scarf in the center of a circle of chairs. After the children and I had seated ourselves, I called their attention to the book that contains God's story and ours. After a few moments of looking at the Bible in silence, I invited them to pray with me verse 105 from Psalm 119: "Your word, O Lord, is a light to guide me."

Then I told them that each of us, beginning with me, would hold the Bible open to that verse on the open palms of our hands, raise it upward in an attitude of prayer and say aloud, "Your word, O Lord, is a light to guide me." As the Bible moved from child to child, each praying the psalm verse, the experience took the form of an undulating wave and a mantra. Admittedly there were a few breaks in the rhythm and an occasional stumbling on the verse, but the prayer was such that the children sat in silence after I had replaced the book on the scarf. I reluctantly broke into their silence so we could prepare for dismissal.

My reasons for enthroning the Bible in every class are these:

• I believe that the Bible is a primary source of faith, is the word of God, and is a strong and visible sign of God's presence.

• Most children and young people have an innate sense that the Bible is a special book and are open to activities that develop their relationship to and use of it.

• Having used the Bible consistently in my religion classes for years, I have come to depend upon it as a significant presence. I would find it as difficult to teach religion without it as to teach without students.

Guided Imagery Meditation

Another form of Bible-based prayer that I find helpful with children and youth of all ages is guided meditation. Lessons in many religion textbooks center on a story from the scriptures. The biblical story may do many things within the lesson, one of which is to be a source of prayer. Guided meditation can be a meaningful way to help children get into the images and spirit of a Bible story. I have had a considerable amount of success with guiding children into meditating on Jesus, using stories from the gospels.

An example: The story is Jesus healing Bartimaeus, the blind man (Mk 10:46-52). I begin by helping them to become completely quiet. I ask them also to close their eyes. Then I invite them to join Jesus who is walking along the road with his disciples. I invite them to be one of the disciples. As they are walking along, sometimes beside Jesus, sometimes behind him, others join them. Jesus seems always happy to see and welcome anyone who wants to be with them. As they are walking along on this particular day they hear a man calling out, "Jesus, help me!"

Some of the people, maybe including you, go to the man and tell him not to shout at Jesus like that. You beg him to be quiet. You also notice that the man is blind and this makes you concerned that he might take up Jesus' attention and time. But the man opens his mouth as wide as he can and shouts even louder, "Jesus, help me."

Jesus stops. You all stop, too, and look at Jesus, wondering what he is going to do about the man who is begging for help. Then Jesus looks right at you and says, "Bring him to me." You hesitate for a second but you quickly go to the man and tell him to get up because Jesus wants to see him. The man smiles, throws his coat on the ground, and moves toward Jesus. Everyone is watching. Everyone is very quiet. Then Jesus speaks to the man, asking, "What do you want?" Bartimaeus—that's the blind man's name—says, "I want to *see*, Lord." Jesus looks lovingly at the man, touches his eyes and says, "You believe . . . you are healed."

I pause in complete silence then to allow the children to wonder prayerfully about what they have just seen and heard.

Then I invite them to open their eyes, say a silent prayer of thanks that they can see. I might close the prayer with a petition that our belief in the Lord becomes stronger and stronger. Amen.

Direct Contact With the Bible

Even though the stories or passages from scripture are in the religion text that I am using, I often help the children to find the particular passage in the Bible itself and to read parts of it silently or aloud.

At times I read the passage aloud to them from the Bible while they listen. At other times I invite them to read the story of the lesson from the Bible and work out a dramatization of it or, in small groups illustrate segments of the story which then are put together sequentially.

I feel it is important for the children to have direct contact with the Bible itself, particularly in relation to prayer. Biblical stories in the textbooks or in children's bibles have the

advantage of simpler language and adaptations that include some of the background and context of the story, which is good, but it is vital that the children also experience at least some of the more accessible stories directly from the Bible itself in a prayer context. The textbook stories may then bring clarification and background to the children's overall appreciation of the story. Hopefully the children's frequent contact with the Bible itself will be influential in their continual use and dependence on it throughout their whole lives.

Handling the Bible With Reverence

In directing the children to find a passage, story or prayer in the Bible, we can also tell them that the Bible, because it is God's Book, demands a careful and loving touch. I believe that we need to remind them again and again until it becomes second nature to them. This extends to the way they learn how to pick up the Bible, how they close it and where they place it when they are finished using it. All of this takes time, but I feel it is one of the most significant things that we might do in our religion classes. Engaging the children with the Book in this way over and over again creates a sensory experience of the holiness that is bound within the Bible's pages. The reverent experience itself is prayer.

Processing With the Bible

On occasion I have found a simple procession with the Bible a meaningful prayer. While seemingly more appropriate with younger children, carefully prepared processions may be used with older children as well. The purpose of such a procession is to help the youngsters pray with the Bible in a way that involves their whole bodies. It can add to the students' sense of reverence for the Bible. Further, the procession with the Bible can relate directly with the liturgical procession at the beginning and end of the Eucharist, as the Book is carried reverently to and from the ambo or reading stand.

Here is how I had a successful procession with the Bible in one of my classes. I chose one child to carry the Bible and two children to carry candles. You might prefer to let the children do the selecting themselves. I showed the one how to carry the Bible, holding it up at eye-level or above so others could see it. I showed the other two children how to walk on either side of the Bible. I had the rest of the class line up in twos behind the Bible-carrier and candle-carriers. I showed them all how to stand tall and to walk reverently in an attitude of prayer.

Then we began the procession, singing as we walked slowly around the room with the Bible. Select a song about God's word, ideally one that is used in the local parish church. Have several moments of silence between verses as the procession moves on.

As the leaders arrive at the place where the Bible is to rest, the one carrying the Bible reverently places it open on the spot prepared for it. The candle bearers place a candle on each side of the Bible. Then one by one each child comes up and bows deeply before the Bible, kisses it, or in some other way shows reverence for the book of God's word.

Making a Bible Prayer Book

I often have the children keep journals or create their own books during the year. Making a prayer book of biblical prayers can be a delightful and long-lasting project.

As the children learn prayers from the psalms or other books of the Bible, they can enter them in their personal "Bible Prayer Book." Their books may be simple verbal records of Bible prayers or could be more creative. For example, ask the children to write a brief selection from a psalm as neatly as possible on one page of their books. Then encourage them to place on the facing page a visual image that captures something of the imagery and meaning of the psalm verses. They might draw or paint a picture, or cut out and paste in an appropriate photo, advertisement or work of art that they find in books or other media. Or they might write their own psalm expressing in modern words and images the sentiments and spirit of the psalm on the opposite page.

The "Bible Prayer Book" can be used in class during moments of silent prayer, or when individuals finish an activity before the rest of the class. It can be taken home for private prayer or for family prayer.

In preparing my lessons I am constantly looking out for simple, creative ways to have the children pray from or in relation to the Bible. I do not use the Bible as a teaching tool. That is what my textbook is for. I use it as a word of affirmation, a word of reflection, a word of owning, a word of prayer. The *National Catechetical Directory* supports such a use: "Catechesis encourages people to use the Bible as a source and inspiration for prayer" (#43).

Things to Think About

1. How much of a resource for your own prayer is the Bible? How do you use the Bible to nurture your own prayer life?

2. What are some of your experiences of using the Bible as a source of prayer in your religion classes? What have you learned from those experiences?

3. What fears or reservations, if any, do you have about using the Bible for prayer in your life, in your classes?

Things to Do

1. Begin to "bank" psalm verses or verses of other biblical prayers that you find most meaningful to you. They may be verses you come across in your textbook as you prepare lessons or verses you hear at Sunday Mass or verses that touch you during your personal reading of the Bible. Learn them by heart, and pray them in appropriate moments as circumstances suggest.

2. Make a habit of reading the Bible in relation to your teaching. For example, look up in the Bible the text that is cited or adapted in a lesson of your textbook. Compare the biblical text itself from the Bible with the version in your textbook. Follow up any notes or references your bible gives to help you better understand that text in relation to other biblical texts. Read the whole biblical chapter from which the textbook passage is taken, so you can interpret the text within its context.

3. Get in the habit of reading your bible with a highlighter pen at hand. When you come across a verse that really speaks to you, highlight it. If you notice a key word that seems to recur often, highlight it. In this way you will find it easier to locate favorite texts and become more aware of how certain themes and words run like threads through the whole Bible.

18
Liturgical Prayers and Symbols

During the 1978-79 school year Carl and I were teaching religion to third graders at our parish, Holy Trinity, in Georgetown, Washington, DC. In our class was a lovely little girl, Maura Davitt. She suffered from cystic fibrosis. I was aware of Maura's illness but most of the time I didn't think about it because Maura was so interested in everything that was going on in the class and participated fully. She was not one of the 23 who demanded special attention. I often chatted with her before class began because she was friendly and was often one of the first children to arrive. Something special happened between us because of those moments—something inexplicable but something I will always cherish because it taught me that children are not only in our classes to be taught but to become friends. Almost always before that experience with Maura I rarely dawdled with the children as they arrived. I would mostly tell or show them where they were to sit and would be preoccupied with the business of getting the show on the road, so to speak.

That experience exemplifies some of what I believe about liturgical prayers and symbols. People do something together over and over again which creates an inner change. The change might be one of bonding or it might be one of healing or it might be one of strengthening or it might be one of accepting the way another is, overlooking and even loving the seeming flaws.

I lost this little friend through death when she was a fourth grader. At Maura's funeral I was in a pew with Christina Pfeffer, another child from that particular class, with whom I had become and still am a friend. We were sitting toward the back of the church. When Father Thomas Gavigan, S.J., a dear friend of the children, sprinkled the small coffin with holy water and began praying, "I bless the body of Maura, with the holy water that recalls

113

her baptism of which Saint Paul writes: All of us who were baptized into Christ Jesus were baptized into his death. By baptism into his death we were buried together with him, so that just as Christ was raised from the dead by the glory of the Father, we too might live a new life. For if we have been united with him by likeness to his death, so shall we be united with him by likeness to his resurrection," Christina stood up on the pew and stretched herself as much as she could so that she could see what Father was doing and hear what he was saying.

She could see well and hear easily as Father Gavigan placed the white pall over the casket and prayed, "On the day of her baptism, Maura put on Christ. In the day of Christ's coming, may she be clothed with glory."

I wasn't surprised at Christina's interest in what was happening during this opening part of the funeral liturgy and the thought occurred to me how teachable a moment that is for children. The connection between what happens both symbolically and really at baptism and at the time of our death is made during the rites of baptism and the funeral liturgy and when children are actually at the scene of both they can make the connection and have some understanding. These sacred moments in the life of the parish community should be seen as privileged teaching as well as worshipping times for our children. They are much more significant, I feel, than are those in a class in which only pictures and words are used to tell the same story.

Children are taught often and with care about the sacramental moments of baptism, confirmation, Eucharist, reconciliation, anointing of the sick, marriage and holy orders, but the actual experience, either through watching or active participation, connects the children more deeply with the sacraments' significance and efficacy. Both sacramental participation and formal instruction are needed in the faith and prayer education of our young. We should be as much concerned about the one as the other. Too often I feel we religious educators depend too much on textbooks and the classroom.

The key is to link as clearly as possible what the children experience in the liturgy and what they learn about liturgy in their classes. Here are some examples of how I try to do that.

Sunday Mass

The most important liturgical celebration in a Catholic Christian's life is the eucharistic liturgy, the Mass. For the Eucharist to have much effect on children it has to be an "always part of their lives" from infancy onward. Some might disagree with this conviction of mine, but my experience suggests that bringing children and liturgical prayer together again and again and again, on an every Sunday or Saturday evening basis, builds a liturgical pattern, a liturgical sense, perhaps primitive, into their subconscious as well as their conscious being. I believe that children who worship on a regular basis with their families may become owners of a faith tradition which provides sustenance and meaning during times of confusion and during times when their spirits hunger for God. I believe, too, that children who have a history of worshipping in their lives possess an added dimension in their personalities. Prayer somehow enhances.

Catechists normally have little role in whether their students take part in Sunday

Mass. That is primarily a parental responsibility. Still, catechists need to make every effort to help children understand the Mass, relating their classes as much as possible to the actual parish liturgical celebrations. For example:

- Describe and explain the *parts of the Mass.*

- Teach and pray appropriate *prayers* from the eucharistic liturgy, like the Sign of the Cross, "I confess to Almighty God" (Confiteor), "Lord have mercy," (Kyrie), "Glory to God" (Gloria), "Profession of Faith" (Creed), "Holy, Holy, Holy" (Sanctus), "Memorial Acclamation," "Lord's Prayer," "Lamb of God" (Agnus Dei), "Lord, I am not worthy" and "Blessing."

- Let the children experience the *vestments*, their shape and color, and the *vessels* such as the chalice and the paten. If possible, have one of the priests demonstrate putting on the vestments, explaining the symbolism of each one as he does so.

- Relate the *crucifix*, a key symbol, with the central meaning of the Mass. Give the children a crucifix of their own as something concrete that links them with the mystery when they are not actually worshipping.

- Read and talk about the Sunday *readings* so that there is a familiarity with the word when they hear the readings again during Mass.

- Sing and study *hymns* used at the Sunday Eucharist.

- Spend time in the local *church* or school *chapel* with the children and teach them about the *altar*, the *symbols* that may be carved into the altar table or on the tabernacle—nearly always eucharistic symbols, the *ambo*—used for reading and proclaiming God's word—and any symbols on it, the *windows*, which often have a picture of the Last Supper or other eucharistic scene, and the *tabernacle.*

- Share with the children *Mass books* that have been prepared specifically for children. Help them learn how to use these books during Mass without letting them distract from participation in the actual celebration.

Most of the better religion textbooks contain the prayers of the Mass in lessons where they fit and also suggest ways to help the children learn about what is going on during the Eucharist and how to participate meaningfully.

Class Masses

One thing Carl and I always do at least once during the class year is have a class Mass. We plan far enough in advance so the children can invite their families to come for the Mass, and can recruit a priest of their choice for the celebration.

We take some time during the weeks preceding the class Mass to invite the children's active participation in planning the Mass. They select readings (where this is appropriate), hymns, and ministers (the priest, lectors, singers, and others). They design the environment, since we like to have the class Mass in the classroom where we have class during the year. They make any symbols and decorations, and prepare invitations.

Our experience has been that this class Mass, involving the children and their families, is a high point of each class year.

Liturgical Symbols

Liturgy is essentially *symbolic* action. There are many symbols in our children's memory. Very early they can identify a symbol that they see and tell what it means. When Angela was two she pointed to a red heart on a valentine and gave me a hug.

The challenge and task for religion teachers with regard to symbols is to fill the children's memories with them so that as they go through life they will recognize and be continually in communion with the sacred and the mystery of God and believing.

The *fish*, an early church symbol meaning Christ, the *butterfly*, a symbol of resurrection, new life, the *dove*, a symbol of the Holy Spirit, a *lamb*, another symbol of Christ, a *candle*, a symbol of Christ's light eclipsing the darkness of evil and sin, *bread* and *wine*, symbols of Christ's body and blood are only a few of the symbols that our children need to have in their memories. Samuel Johnson said, "The true art of memory is the art of attention." The more attention we give to symbols and their meanings in our religious education of children, the more, I believe, will their attention on the sacred be held.

The children's appreciation of liturgical symbols rests on the fostering of the symbolic or sacramental *imagination.* So much contemporary culture and education is oriented to the scientific, quantitative, measurable and factual that religious educators sometimes need to foster qualities of creativity and imagination. Water as a liturgical symbol in baptism rests on the *natural symbolism* of water, symbolizing life and at the same time symbolizing death. This symbolism can be appreciated by intentionally *experiencing* water (so common a part of daily life we easily take it for granted), enjoying it, feeling its refreshing power, wondering at its potential for destruction. The experience can be nurtured and deepened through poetry, story, creative writing, drawing and music, for example. Catechists are in a privileged position to foster an appreciation of the symbolic meaning of water and other liturgical symbols.

But water used in baptism comes laden with a whole other layer of symbolic meaning, its *biblical symbolism.* In the memory of Jews and Christians water recalls God's creative act in making the world, God saving humankind through the flood, God freeing the Hebrew slaves through the waters of the Reed Sea, God granting a promised land to God's people crossing the waters of the Jordan River. The biblical symbolism of water recalls their rivers of water that enlivened the Garden of Eden, the streams giving life to trees along its shores, the living water flowing from the rock in the desert, from the Temple in Jerusalem, from the pierced heart of the Crucified, from the Throne and the Lamb in the New Jerusalem. It is the living water Jesus promised the Samaritan woman at Jacob's well. It calls to mind the Holy Spirit.

We have the opportunity to share this richness of *biblical* and *natural* symbolism with the children in our catechesis.

Paraliturgies

Another way of linking catechesis and the church's liturgy is through prayer services that draw upon some of the principles and elements of liturgical worship, particularly the Liturgy of the Hours, while remaining more flexible than the liturgy itself. These prayer services may be developed in relation to a particular lesson in the curriculum, a special event or celebration, a doctrinal theme, a saint's feastday, a birthday or almost any occasion.

Paraliturgies may be quite simple or elaborate. In their simplest form they contain four elements that reflect prayer traditions going back to the church's earliest days:

- *reading* a biblical text;
- *singing* an appropriate hymn;
- *praying* a related prayer;
- *doing* a symbolic action.

More elaborate prayer services may add to those elements an introduction or procession, additional readings from the Bible and other sources, more hymns, different kinds of prayers—silent meditation, intercessions, litanies, acclamations—a variety of actions, and a conclusion. Even in elaborate services, however, it is good to keep the central theme and feeling simple.

Paraliturgies allow for maximum participation of all students as well as for great flexibility and creativity.

Liturgical Hours and Seasons

The church divides time into liturgical moments. Jesus and Mary followed the Jewish practice of praying at three special times each day—morning, midday and evening—and celebrated the annual Jewish feastdays. The early followers of Jesus did likewise, but adapted the times and feasts to reflect their new faith. Over the years the church created what we now call the Liturgy of the Hours and the Liturgical Year.

Our catechesis can help our children gradually learn the rhythm of the church's prayer cycles on a daily and seasonal basis. We can encourage them to pray in the morning on arising and at night before falling asleep.

The Advent wreath, for example, is a seasonal object, as is the Jesse tree. Both of these appeal to children. I remember a year when I decided that since there was an Advent wreath in church where we assembled for Sunday worship, and since many of the parents had adopted the practice in their home preparation for Christmas, I was not going to use it in my Advent classes.

Fortunately for the children I had to go out of town and my co-teacher took over the second class of the Advent season. He built an Advent wreath with the children and used it both as a teaching tool and as a focus for prayer. The children liked it so much they lost no time in informing me how much they had enjoyed their last class and went on and on about the Advent wreath. Needless to say, even though the following was the last class before Christmas, we had an Advent wreath.

We sometimes underestimate the children's readiness and appreciation for such rituals or neglect them in our concern with teaching what seems more essential. Yet the repeated seasonal rituals enable the children to enter into the church's liturgical seasons.

Things to Think About

1. What is your own experience of the church's liturgy? How meaningful for your life is Sunday Mass? the other sacraments?

2. How have you felt about the liturgical changes since Vatican Council II? Have you found them personally helpful? Why? Why not?

3. How conscious are you of relating your lessons to the church's official worship?

Things to Do

1. Go through your schedule of classes for the year with a look at a liturgical calendar. Note on your class schedule the dates of major seasons like Advent and Lent, important feasts like Christmas and Easter and other holy days, as well as feasts of saints you feel are important for your children. Then do the same with an eye on the parish calendar. Note down important liturgical dates like first communion, first reconciliation, confirmation, key celebrations in the RCIA (if your parish has a catechumenate program), feast of the parish patron saint and other feasts. Each week glance over the parish bulletin for notices of liturgical events like weddings, funerals or the anointing of the sick. Then plan your classes with the intention of relating them with the more important liturgical seasons, feasts and sacramental celebrations.

2. Begin to collect resources helpful in expanding the symbolic imagination of your students. For example, keep your eyes open for strong visual images. Sometimes ads have powerful images relating to water, oil, bread, wine, wedding rings. Sometimes, too, in the news media striking photos are published that reveal the meaning and deep feelings associated with symbols or symbolic actions that are used in the church's liturgy. Many composers have created beautiful "water" music and moving love songs. Contemporary rock hits, at times, touch on the same themes and symbols as does the liturgy. Gather any poems or stories that provide insight into sacramental symbols. The more you can use real life imagery and sources, the more you will find the children interested in the church's liturgical symbolism and celebrations.

3. Recall and ponder the symbols and rituals that particularly appeal to you during a liturgical season such as Advent or Lent. Are there some that have been culturally a part of your family that would add to the children's experience and expand their awareness of special aspects of the season? Plan ways to make them part of your classes.

19
Traditional Prayers

The traditional Catholic prayers were, for years, the only prayers most Catholic children learned. Both at home and in religion classes children were expected to know by memory such prayers as the Sign of the Cross, the Our Father, the Hail Mary, the Doxology or Glory Be, the Morning Offering, the Angelus, the Apostles Creed, the Act of Contrition, Grace at Meals and the Acts of Faith, Hope and Love.

I have vivid memories of my preparation, as a second grader, for first confession and first communion. We spent whole classes in which all we did was recite aloud, one after the other, prayers that had to be memorized. And not minding it! That was the way it was. And, learn them we did! Memorizing the basic Catholic prayers was an important part of our sacramental preparation.

As a religion teacher myself I later did much the same with the children I prepared for first confession and communion. But then in the '60s we began giving less attention to these traditional Catholic prayers. We taught them in religion classes but memorization was not always required.

At the same time, perhaps even earlier, families were no longer teaching their children these prayers. Many rarely prayed them in their homes and more and more children didn't know any of the traditional prayers by heart. Some Catholic families explored other, more creative ways to pray at home; others simply lost the habit of family prayer. So the children more often than not came to religion class without familiarity with these prayers.

In recent years, during the '70s and '80s, there has been a sense of loss in the Catholic community regarding traditional prayers and a resurgence has occurred. Religious education programs now not only print these prayers at the back of religion textbooks but build them generously into lessons throughout the year.

Memorizing traditional prayers, learning them by heart, has again become an expected and accepted part of the religious education of children and young people. The *National Catechetical Directory* mentions the following prayers that should be known by all Catholics: Apostles' Creed, Sign of the Cross, the Lord's Prayer, Hail Mary, Glory Be to the Father, Acts of Faith, Hope and Charity, Act of Contrition (#143, 176e).

Why Teach Traditional Prayers?

Let me cite a few good reasons for learning these prayers:

• Prayers, more than abstract belief statements, provide an identity with a community, a religious tradition, a church.

• Commonly known prayers allow children to pray with adults as well as with other children in the Catholic community.

• The content of many of our traditional prayers is central to the story of faith that we hope our children will not only learn but will own. Ancient Christians used to say *lex orandi, lex credendi*, "the rule of prayer is the rule of belief," or perhaps less literally but more simply, "how people pray shows what they believe." Traditional prayers help preserve beliefs.

• The prayers that children have locked in their memories may provide solace at times, courage at others, and connect them with a ray of hope when they most need it. This may be a reason that seems to border on the ideal; however, I have found myself praying the Our Father and the Hail Mary at lonesome times, at worrisome times and at times of great sadness. The long-familiar prayers seem to surface spontaneously and provide me with just enough help to make it through.

• The requirement to know, by heart, certain traditional prayers is important to many parents and religion teachers who want their children and students to "know their prayers." Because this is a priority on the part of many Catholic parents, there is a willingness to assist their children in the memorization process at home because the time that children have for religious education in the once-a-week setting is too limited to do much memorizing on a regular basis.

With these reasons in mind I will share some of the ways I have found to help children learn the traditional Catholic prayers by heart, learn something of their meaning and actually pray these prayers.

Memorizing the Prayers

Memorizing prayers is not praying them, but is a preliminary help to praying them in a meaningful way. I have found several ways to help my students learn these prayers by heart.

Involve parents.   Often I have successfully included a prayer that I hope the children will learn by heart in the body of a letter to parents. I tell the parents what we did in class, and share with them how that prayer was part of the instruction. I then ask them to assist their children in learning the prayer by heart. I do this, at the most, only about four times during the school year. In the letter I suggest praying the prayer several times during the week at meals, at bedtime, in the car when they are alone with the children. I suggest putting the prayer on the refrigerator or in another place where it can be seen frequently.

Visual helps.   Another thing that I have done is put the prayer on a narrow piece of tagboard, decorate it and give one to each child, suggesting that it be used as a bookmark in a book they are reading. Or I have the children make their own prayer bookmarks.

Sometimes I hang up a poster containing the words of one of these prayers. Some textbook publishers offer such attractive prayer posters as part of their curriculum. I also have the children make large posters of the traditional prayers for hanging up during class, rotating prayers on a regular basis.

With younger children I have made a chart with each child's name along the left hand side and three or four traditional prayers named at the top, for example, with first graders, the Sign of the Cross, the Our Father and the Hail Mary. I explain the chart to them and tell them that a gold star will be placed behind their names when they can pray those prayers by heart. On occasion during class I will ask who knows a prayer on the chart, give the child an opportunity to pray it aloud and place the gold star after his or her name.

Creative booklet.   Another activity, a project one, is the creation of a prayer booklet in which each child draws pictures and prints phrases of the prayer on each page of the booklet. This takes a bit of time, but in a parochial school setting this could be continued in an art class.

Learning the Meaning of These Prayers

Memorizing prayers needs to go hand in hand with learning the meaning of those same prayers. We do not want just rote memory of prayers the children do not understand. Children's unwitting mistakes in the recitation of a prayer like the Our Father may be humorous, but all they reveal is that the child does not grasp the meaning of the prayer. So I try to give considerable attention to explaining each word or phrase on the level of the children's present ability to understand. Fortunately the modern textbooks are planned to facilitate the learning of the meaning of these traditional Catholic prayers. Here are some methods I've found useful.

Learn within meaningful context.   The textbooks usually place the prayers in lessons that relate to their meaning. For example, in a lesson on Mary, particularly on the Annunciation or Visitation, you could expect to find the Hail Mary since it is taken from the biblical accounts of those two events in Mary's life. So, too, the Our Father might be expected in a lesson on God, our Father, or in a lesson on prayer, in which the gospel account of Jesus teaching this prayer to his disciples is read.

In this way, by relating the prayer with its origins in the Bible, or with a theme that suggests something of the prayer's meaning, you can help the children learn, at their level of understanding, the meaning of a traditional prayer they are learning by heart.

Unfolding meaning.   Further, the same prayers are part of the lessons in several of the grade levels. For example, the Sign of the Cross, learned originally in first grade, may be retaught and prayed in Grade Two and continue to be part of the praying in the succeeding grades.

So, too, the Our Father, Hail Mary and Apostles' Creed might appear explicitly as part of lessons in most of the grades. Other of the traditional prayers are also taught and prayed at different grade levels and are repeated at significant times during the year. The intent is to build the traditional prayers into the lessons in a way that makes them part of the mosaic of the children's religious and faith life as Catholics.

While the textbooks provide much guidance, I find myself trying to be even more conscious of opportunities and techniques of helping my students enrich their understanding of these important prayers.

Praying These Prayers

It is important that the children actually pray the traditional Catholic prayers in class in various settings throughout their religious education. To some extent the textbooks facilitate this by their repeated inclusion of these prayers in lessons in each grade level.

Prayer Books. I often guide the children in creating their own prayer books. Some textbooks provide samples or tear-out booklets that can be helpful for starting such a project. Their prayer books may include the text of the traditional prayers together with, for example, their personal reflections on each prayer, and/or visual images that they feel speak to the prayer—drawings, photos, ads, art. I encourage the children also to write and include original prayers in their prayer book, for example, in relation to one of the traditional prayers. We then use the completed prayer books for praying in subsequent classes.

At times I give the children a prayer book as a gift, for example the one Carl and I wrote, *Living Water: Prayers of Our Heritage* (Paulist: 1978). I usually give it to the children as a Christmas gift and ask them to bring it with them to succeeding classes. We use it frequently during the classes after Christmas and the rest of the year.

Music and song. I find that music can be helpful in praying some of the more common traditional prayers. Most parishes use one of the popular musical versions of the Our Father. Singing this basic Christian prayer not only adds freshness and variety to praying the Lord's Prayer but links our prayer in class more consciously with the parish or school eucharistic liturgy. The Hail Mary, usually in Latin, *Ave Maria*, set to music by several well-known composers, can be used to enrich the praying of this most popular Marian prayer. Musical versions of other traditional prayers may also be used effectively.

Gesture. Involving the whole body in praying these common prayers is an excellent way to bring new life to the children's prayer. I sometimes use gestures I find in published materials or pick up at workshops. I have also found that children seem to enjoy working out their own gestures and are quite capable at it. Doing so can be much more meaningful because the children bring their own understanding of the prayer into the creation of the gestures. Gesturing the prayer helps make the praying of it more expressive and meaningful.

Alternative prayer techniques. One of the problems with praying traditional prayers is the tendency to routine, thoughtless praying. To combat this I draw upon the experience of prayerful Christians of the past, like St. Ignatius Loyola, to engage the children in different ways of praying these oft-prayed prayers.

For example, Ignatius suggests at times praying the Our Father very slowly and silently in harmony with the pattern of deep, relaxed breathing. Pray only one word with each slow breath, letting the mind, heart and imagination dwell on that single word. This method is relaxing and contemplative. It can greatly enrich the praying of any of the basic Catholic prayers.

Ignatius suggests yet another method. Become relaxed and dwell on the first word, say of the Lord's Prayer, for as long as you find it meaningful. For example, take the first word of the prayer, *our*, and stay with it as long as it speaks to you. Only then move on to the next word. This method allows still greater penetration of your consciousness by the images, ideas and feelings of the prayer.

There are many ways in which traditional prayers can become part of our religion classes and thereby part of the children's developing faith life. It takes a bit of imagination, an awareness of how traditional prayers are part of the lessons in your textbook and a commitment to praying these prayers as well as others on a regular basis.

Things to Think About

1. What part do the traditional Catholic prayers play in your own prayer life? Why?

2. What ways have you found to make these commonplace prayers more meaningful in your own prayer?

3. Why do you feel these prayers are an important part of the content of catechesis for children?

4. What would we lose if these prayers were forgotten and no longer used by Catholics?

Things to Do

1. While praying the Creed and the Lord's Prayer during Mass, rejoice in the beauty and the depth of these prayers, so central to our Catholic Christian tradition.

2. Discover how many of the traditional prayers you know by heart. Perhaps memorize one or two more from time to time.

3. Before instructing the children in your class about one of the prayers, experiment with creative ways of both teaching and praying it.

20
Writing

Writing, more than most activities that we do with children in learning situations, requires searching within oneself. We need to draw upon personal experience unless the writing merely reports on another person or an event. Writing asks us to leave off superficial musings and discover deep down thoughts and feelings and bring them to the surface. Writing enables the writer to discover inner truth and make it visible. It can reveal patterns in a person's life and it can motivate toward developing or changing the patterns. This is why journaling has become so popular in recent years. Taking time daily to write is a way for people to get in touch with their ongoing stories and to get better control of how those stories will continue. Writing is wondrous in making one aware of unexamined, really unknown thoughts, feelings and knowledge. Oftentimes we are aware that the subconscious harbors a wealth of gleanings from experiences and on-the-run reflections about them, but we never take the time or the means to sort them out and bring them to the surface. Writing is one of the best means of doing this. It is a powerful tool—even for young children!

The following story is an example. Two years ago when our goddaughter, Angela, was seven, she decided to write about Jesus for an assignment in her second grade class. Angela had been hearing about Jesus all her young years—at home, with us, in church, in CCD, and occasionally on TV. But she had never before tried to put it all together in relation to her young life. Here is what she wrote totally on her own.

Jesus Newborn Baby

Jesus' parents' names are Mary and Joseph. He was born in Bethlehem in a stable. Lots of animals were in the stable and kings and shepherds came to visit him there. His dad was a carpenter. His mom prayed a lot because she was worried about what would happen when he grew up.

He grew up and helped lots of people who were sick, sad, blind, crippled, and poor.

Even though people were mean to him he was never mean.

People didn't like what he said and did so they killed him by hanging him on a cross, but he did not stay dead.

I am a follower of Jesus because he did great things. My parents and godparents are followers of Jesus too.

I learn about and pray to Jesus in church, at home and in Sunday School.

At home I have a book about Jesus called <u>I Walk With Jesus.</u> My favorite story in it is about the time Jesus walked with two men on a road and they did not know that Jesus was walking with them.

His parents were proud of him because he grew up to be such a nice man.

I love Jesus. He is my friend.

In every religion class that I teach, the children write, not just once but twice or more during the time that we're together. Over the years I have found that if I just depend upon oral responses or reflections on the content at hand the return is, at best, mediocre and at worst, superficial. Then, too, oral responses willingly come from the few, rather than the many, and I am forced to beg, cajole and demand responses from the others.

Writing consistently gets everyone in the class working on a question or a topic and when it comes time to share, everyone usually has something at hand to contribute. Because writing, even a paragraph or two, takes some discipline, not all the children enjoy it. Nearly every time, no matter that we do it in every session, some of the same children will sit, pencil in hand, paper untouched, pleading that they can't think of anything. My response is helpful insofar as I suggest a variety of ways in which they might place the question to their inner selves and discover an answer that they have. I also make a point that they know far more about the question than they know they know at this moment of resistance. I encourage them to start writing whatever comes to mind about it. Some groups can be more easily led in the art of writing in a way that brings the inner truth to the surface. The group of sixth graders that I have this year are much more resistant. Often what they write is much less revelatory and less in touch with that truth I feel they possess but I never give up because so far every one of them, at one time or another, has written something that is memorable both to themselves and to me.

Writing and Praying

What does this mean in relationship to prayer? It's curious to me how often in the everyday writing by columnists and reporters a prayer will evolve that expresses the deepest feelings about an issue that the writer has. For example, in the *Washington Post*, in a column entitled "A Town Weary of Death Endures Yet Another," Courtland Milloy, the writer, ended his column with what I call a prayer. He writes about the death of Sterling Brown, the District's poet laureate, "He left us at a most inopportune moment, Lord. His death may have freed him from the agony of cancer, but it has deprived us of a very courageous man, one whose gift for caring and sharing is so desperately needed these days."

Writing Prayers

Written prayers can be strong and tangible personal outcries to God about events, needs and feelings. Many of the 150 psalms are this kind of written prayer.

Written prayers can be expressions of personal desires for a more loving way and the help of God in bringing this about. For example, in one of my sixth grade classes I asked each student to write a prayer that expresses his or her desire to help build a world of justice, peace and love. I was both delighted and amazed at their written prayers which are as follows:

Dear God, Please make more peace on earth more friendship and more health. Please make it loving with trust and care and love that's coming from your heart. A M E N

Helen Martin

Dear God, please keep our world be safe and free and make us know what is right or wrong. If it is meant let it be. If it can be helped, help. Help those who need help. Help us love and know to love you. Keep us together in our family.

Courtney Carr

Dear God, Will you please give help to our new president and give him help to govern our great nation of ours. Give him confidence to help and guide us. Amen

Matt Spaeder

Dear God, Please help others in need of money, shelter, education, and respect. Free the world of alcohol, drugs, and all other things that harm us. Clear people's minds of wrongdoing like murder, and bring in a mind of peace, love and friendship.

Tommy Skapars

Dear God Let the world be free from any kind of prejudice, violence, cruelty, and injustice. Help us be more understanding about peoples feelings and thoughts.

Gabriela Meza

Dear God, Please help the homeless, drug addicts, & alcoholics and people all over the world who are suffering. Amen

Suzanne Reigle

Dear God, Please help the world be a safer, more peaceful and free place, God. The world is so full of evil and cruelty, and I know that even I am like that sometimes. Please help me try my best to be a caring person, and please help the rest of the world be full of good, too. I believe in you, and trust that you will help the world. Thank you.

Jennie Chu

Dear God Please keep our world safe and happy and peaceful. Help people stay together and love each other very much. Please keep the Russians and the United States peaceful forever. Amen

Nicole Asmar

Lord, Lord where have we gone wrong why are there people living on the streets help those who need food and home to a better and more respectable lives.

Leigh Corrigan

Dear Lord, Please Give our President the power and strength to abolish nuclear arms and have peace worldwide. Put an end to drugs and war. And make everyone nicer to everybody else.

John Ismay

Dear Lord, I hope that one day everyone would live in a world full of Peace. I hope There would be justice throughout. And equal rights for every one.

Michael Preuss

Prayer Gifts/Spiritual Bouquets

Written prayers can be expressions of wishes for the welfare of another. At Christmas time I always have my students write prayer gifts. I like to tell this story about what happened one year with a sixth grader who was so consistently disruptive that by Christmas time I was about to give up on him. When I invited the children to write prayer gifts I was nearly shocked that he didn't display his usual disdain and got right to the business of creating his gift. He not only wrote one prayer but two and they were for his mother. I have kept copies of both of his prayers because they touched me so much and made a great difference in how I felt and reacted to him following that class. His prayers changed my feelings toward him which in turn changed his feelings toward me and from then on our behavior with each other improved greatly.

These are his two prayers:

Dear God, Please help me be kind to my family especially my mother who is pregnant and help her have a very healthy baby and that baby believe in you.

Dear God, please help my mother have a very healthy and happy baby, I hope the baby has a good education and loves people very much and people love the baby very much. I also hope the baby is a girl. AMEN

Writing prayer gifts is not new in our tradition. One of the most familiar ways in the past was the making up of *spiritual bouquets*. This practice is still around, although not nearly as much as when I was a child. For a long time I worried that I would burn in purgatory for all the promises I made on spiritual bouquets that I never kept. There was something about that way of giving a gift that brought out complete generosity and it was not unusual for me to promise 500 rosaries, 1000 ejaculations, 100 Our Fathers and 365 Masses. I was a compulsive spiritual bouquet giver. Such numbers and prayers were not only on one spiritual bouquet, they were promised every time spiritual bouquets were made—Mother's and Father's Day, Christmas and Easter time, birthdays and anniversaries, and as a healing expression when someone was ill. I suspect other children who were making spiritual bouquets, as I was, may have been more responsible in keeping their promises. In those instances spiritual bouquets were a great gift. One thing that writing spiritual bouquets did for us was make us keenly aware that praying for another was a good and desirable thing to do. And, often I would remember that I had made a spiritual bouquet and although I couldn't remember how many prayers I still owed, I would pray some of the prayers for that person.

Original Prayers

Today writing original prayers is part of the religious education of most of our children and besides the kinds mentioned above, there are the following:

- The writing of psalms
- Writing prayers expressing sorrow for sins
- Writing litanies
- Taking words like *thanks*, *praise*, *faith* and *love* and creating a prayer out of them
- Reflecting on a picture and writing a short prayer about it
- Writing prayer intentions like the Prayer of the Faithful that is prayed during Mass
- Writing thank you prayers to God and Jesus
- Re-writing a traditional prayer in own words
- Writing a letter to God
- Writing signatures on a prayer banner
- Writing personal prayers to the Holy Spirit
- Writing short personal prayers to pray every day
- Writing prayers in small groups and placing them on a prayer poster
- Writing on slips of paper names of people to pray for
- Writing a personal prayer to God that expresses what God means and is like
- Writing ways of remembering Jesus during Lent
- Writing a prayer asking God's help in keeping a specific commandment

- Writing prayers that express sorrow for hurting someone and ask God's forgiveness
- Writing dreams for a better world and adding a petition like, "Jesus, help this dream come true."

These are ways that I have used over the years in writing prayers with children. There are certainly many other ways. Once it is decided that writing prayers is a worthwhile and deepening activity, these are some hints that can assure success.

Some Helpful Hints

As part of the directions to the children about the kind of prayer they are to write, invite them to become quiet, to place themselves consciously in God's presence. Help them to appreciate that God initiates prayer in us and we need moments of quiet and silence to get in touch with the prayer that is going on within.

Expect each child to write a prayer. I often pray silently for the children while they are writing or thinking about what they will write, so that the prayer in each one will come forth. Do not become anxious if some of the children don't begin writing immediately, but quietly support, encourage and give a child who seems dry whatever assistance is needed, short of writing the prayer. The important attitude for you is to believe that each one will write a prayer. Communicate that belief by your show of quiet confidence which can be exhibited by sitting quietly in their midst, writing a prayer of your own or simply walking from one to the other, nodding your head in acknowledgment of what is appearing on different children's papers. This expectancy and presence is necessary each time the children are engaged in writing prayers. Gradually they will expect this as much from you as you expect written prayers to come from them. I have found that, of all the things that I have children write, prayers come easiest. And, even with the most resisting of groups, the return is nearly 100 percent.

The prayers that the children write always become the prayer of that session. If a child reveals a strong desire not to pray aloud what he or she has written, I allow that child to pass, but passing is a rare option in my classes. After the first couple of times when the children realize that praying is what the group is doing, with no comments by anyone including their teacher, they relax and participate. I have found that this is a significant way to use the prayers they have written. They're often both impressed and inspired by the prayers that came out of themselves and each time after, the writing of prayers becomes easier and more expressive of their inner feelings, thoughts and relationship with God, Jesus and the Holy Spirit.

If the prayer is not going to be written in their textbooks, as is the case sometimes, I often decorate the paper on which the prayer is to be written with a border or a symbol or a scriptural phrase that is part of the lesson. This, I feel, enhances the experience. It says that this is not an ordinary activity.

I recommend writing prayers in one out of four classes. It is a vital way to help children grow in a deep sense and ownership of God's praying presence within themselves and to equip them with a knowledge that they have a personal power to pray about anything in their own unique way, drawing upon their own personal relationship with a loving, caring, very present God. Sometimes I enourage the children to keep their prayers in a special book, so that they create their own prayer book for present and future use.

Things to Think About

1. What has been your personal experience of writing prayers? How helpful have you found the practice?

2. What do you feel is the value of writing prayers?

3. What has been your experience of having the children write prayers?

Things to Do

1. Try writing prayers yourself. Plan to set aside a few minutes each day for a week or two at a time when you can count on being undisturbed. Take a pen, or use your typewriter or computer, and put into words a prayer that expresses your present feelings and situation. Write your prayer in any form you wish, not putting any limits or restrictions on yourself. Just let your heart dictate the words and the form. After one or two weeks read over your daily prayers and consider what you learn from the experience.

2. To become more familiar with traditional Judaeo-Christian prayer forms, try writing your own prayers according to the form and structure of traditional prayers. You might take a psalm you like. Then write your own prayer modeled on it, with the same number of verses, patterns and structure. Do the same with a liturgical prayer from the Mass, for example the Opening Prayer that comes just after the *Gloria*.

3. Introduce more frequent writing of prayers in your classes. At first encourage the children to write freely, selecting their own words and structure. Later introduce them to one or two typical psalm patterns and the typical liturgical prayer pattern and let them write prayers patterned on these models.

21
Drawing and Painting

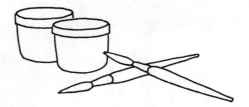

I often find myself thinking about a group of seventh graders who were very skilled with words but resisted using them much in our religion classes. Granted, they didn't actually refuse to respond orally and in writing, but they gave us many signals that they preferred to draw, to illustrate. At first we didn't pick up the signals because we subconsciously believed that drawing was a good activity for primary, even middle grade children, but hardly for young people in junior high. Finally one evening during class Kristin asked, "Why can't we draw what we see and feel rather than write a story about it?" The others quickly backed Kristin's question with a resounding, "Yeaaaah!" Carl pondered the situation for a moment and answered, "Fine!" Then he queried them a bit for some suggestions on how they wanted to do the picturing. They suggested a chalkboard mural. In groups of two they drew a mural that was seven panels wide and revealed far more than we thought they knew and certainly more than we had taught or expected. After the mural was completed they were eager to use words to tell the story that it visualized and more.

Drawing became one of our most frequently used activities with that class and all of us learned much together. One drawing of the Pentecost story (they were preparing for the sacrament of confirmation) was startling in what it revealed of the attitudes in the apostles as the Holy Spirit descended upon them.

Frankly I had never thought of how differently each one must have felt on receiving the Spirit at that momentous event until I studied Steven's drawing. My image had been one of each person looking upward in exactly the same position with a flame nestling a bit above his or her head. But even more than having my image of that event enhanced, both Carl and I were amazed at how much was inside that boy's heart and the depth of his awareness of that story. He had never revealed much of what he knew and felt in writing or talking because he was shy, and his writing ability was far less than his ability to communicate by drawing. Here is Steven De Filippi's drawing.

133

Steven D.

NAME Sophy B.

DRAW A PICTURE
OF SOMEONE PRAYING.
WRITE THE WORDS OF HIS
OR HER PRAYER.

In another religion class—this one with third graders—we asked the children to draw a picture of what they think and feel prayer is. Almost all of them drew themselves praying, some of them in church, some in other settings, such as Jody's drawing of herself praying, included here.

The amazing thing, in this instance, was that they revealed to us that their answer to the question, "What is Prayer?" was different when they drew it than when they wrote an answer to the same question. When they answered the question narratively, most generalized and used words that they had learned as descriptions of prayer, but when they drew an answer to the question, it was something that they or someone else did, something that was part of their lives, something very important and necessary. I can often get the same response with writing but I have to work much harder in engaging them to write from the heart as well as the mind. When they draw answers, often both happens and they are mostly unaware of how comprehensively they have dealt with a question.

Why are drawing and painting important to the task of helping children to believe in prayer, to understand its place in the art of being human, and to ensure that they have in their memory banks a variety of prayers and an awareness that there are many ways to pray?

Importance of Images

Drawing, for the most part, deals with sight, and reveals what has been visually perceived. Children perceive visually before they can explain with words. And visualizing is, for most people, a key step in understanding. Aristotle, a greatly respected philosopher, observed, "The soul never thinks without an image." Albert Einstein, a renowned physicist, declared, "The words or the language, as they are written and spoken, do not seem to play any role in my mechanism of thought." For Aristotle and Einstein, it seems that symbols and images, rather than written words, happened first in their creative thinking.

Drawing, like writing, has the power to bring the inner world out into the open. But there are some important differences. Writing tells us what something is whereas drawing shows it to us. The written word normally addresses the mind first and then the heart whereas a drawing often addresses both at the same time. The written word, if carefully crafted, does not need the imagination to reveal its content, whereas a drawing often is highly dependent upon the imagination of anyone who looks at it. A writer can write sentences without necessarily understanding the content whereas someone who draws a picture to reveal a feeling or belief images something that is embedded inside, that is owned, that is perceived knowledge. Certainly the latter can also be true of someone who writes, while the former can be true of someone who draws. I have heard children using both mediums exclaim, "I didn't know I knew all that."

Just as writing gives children a way to examine what they think, feel and know, so does drawing, but in a different way. Let's reflect on this in relation to drawings that children might do in religion classes. For example, children might be invited to draw a picture of themselves making up to someone that they have hurt in a context wherein they are learning the Act of Contrition or a prayer of sorrow. Drawing pictures of personal attempts to reconcile challenges children to image attitudes that reveal being sorry, and gestures that express regret visually. Often, too, the words, "I'm sorry!", "I didn't mean to hurt you" and "I'll never do that again" show up in the drawings as well. Imaging themselves doing the loving thing can increase their perception of how much they need to be forgiven and how necessary it is for them to forgive. The imaging can be instructive insofar as it teaches that an Act of Contrition, a prayer of sorrow, is not just something that we say, it is also something that we do.

Drawing Prayers

Praying is communicating with God, revealing gratitude, love, trust, faith, dependence, hope. Drawing is a near-perfect way for children to reveal what is in their imaginations about saying thanks, praising, and telling God how much they love, hope, believe and depend upon him. It also enhances these perceptions.

Children, in the process of picturing, do some essentially prayerful things. They pause to wonder about what they are about to draw or they begin immediately a wordless conversation that gradually moves from within to without, forming into lines and shapes that reveal what is felt, believed, appreciated, understood and desired. Once the drawing begins, the conversation often flows easily or there are pauses in which listening seems to be going on. Then a line might be added, the paper might be turned over for a few moments, and finally there is what seems to be an "Amen" as it is handed to the teacher or put aside. Drawing, for many children, can be quieting, restorative, fulfilling, surprising. It is, I believe, often the result of something initiated in them and a response on their part.

Paul wrote to the Christian community at Philippi, "For to me life is Christ" (Phil 1:21). To live as Christ lived is to be a prayerful presence in the world. Children given opportunities to draw themselves doing something that could remind others of Jesus, doing something caring and kind, doing something thoughtful, can be revealing to themselves as well as to others that they understand and maybe will even follow this call in their lives. Being compassionately present to others is a high form of prayer.

Children learn prayers more heartily when they draw interpretations of phrases, when they rewrite them according to their own images.

I have had children draw pictures of their families at Mass. It can be illuminating to children insofar as some of them see for the first time how important an activity this is in their family's life. In talking about their pictures afterwards children have made statements like this, "This is something we do all the time." "Sometimes Mass is boring but I like it that we're all together there." "We do this every week 'cause my Mom says we're Catholics and that's how Catholics pray." "You see me down there. I can't see what's going on." "I just drew my family. They could be anywhere but they're at Mass."

Drawing in religion classes is as instructive to the teacher as it may be to the children. When a child says through his or her drawing that what is going on at Mass can't be seen and therefore there is little knowledge or understanding, we can make a difference by our instruction. We might also make a difference by suggesting to the parents that at times it might be good to participate at Mass closer to the altar table.

Drawing pictures of gospel stories can be praying experiences as well as visual and personal interpretations of biblical events. As children reflect on what is happening in the story, as they spend time picturing in their imaginations what Jesus or others are feeling and doing, as they talk to themselves about what the characters in the story are saying, an interior dialogue goes on that may create association, identification, appreciation, belief, affection and wonder.

Sometimes I suggest that the children make a prayer drawing consisting just of lines and colors, expressing a feeling of praise, thanks, sorrow, or need. This impressionistic approach can be very expressive of the children's inner feelings of prayer.

I have touched on only a few ways of prayerful drawing in religion classes. For others you might ponder the images that you have stored in your memory banks and use them as a resource for inviting your students to draw.

Some Helpful Hints

Finally, I would like to mention some things that I have found helpful when drawing is a part of my religion classes.

Before I build a drawing activity into a lesson plan, I nearly always attempt a drawing of the image myself. My drawing skills are quite limited but I am not concerned about that. My reason for personally doing the kind of drawing I will ask the children to do is to discover, first of all, if what I'm asking them to do is too abstract, if I need to sharpen the directions for the drawing, and secondly, approximately how much time should be allowed both mimimally and maximally. And, thirdly, is the drawing a worthwhile use of time—did anything happen to me while I was doing the drawing? Did it really force me to look more deeply to discover some inner information?

I consider the tools that the children will use for their drawings. Nearly always I try to provide each child with his or her own box of crayons. I have learned that when two or more children are sharing a box, all of them want to use the same color at the same time and will wait for it. This creates an interruption in the process. I also check the condition of the crayons. Children like whole crayons and, to the extent possible, sharp ones. The quality and the size of the drawing paper are other considerations. For young children I use large pieces. As often as possible, I use good quality paper and many times I draw lines to create frames.

Before the children begin to draw I suggest that their drawing fill the page—that they draw generously, that they draw in large, flowing strokes, that they make what they see big enough so that others will be able to see it easily. This is one of the biggest challenges I have had over the years. For some reason that I have not yet figured out most children tend to draw in miniature and often on only a small part of the page, no matter how large it is.

While the children are drawing, I quietly walk from one to the other, pausing briefly, communing silently, and on occasion making an encouraging comment. I usually do this two or three times while the children are working.

When the "masterpieces" are finished, there is always time for the children to share the stories that their drawings tell. This is built into the time allotted for the activity in the lesson plan.

At the end of class I collect the drawings so that I can study them before the next class.

Many times I use one or another to involve the children in a review, to make a connection with what we are doing in the class at hand and at times I have displayed all of them for study before we engage in a new drawing. Later I return them to the children. I have discovered that taking their drawings seriously motivates the children to take the activity seriously. I am amazed at the growth in imaging that regularly occurs from the beginning of the year to the end. And I have found that children, especially older ones, can draw as easily and as fully as they can write, but they need many opportunities. In their school settings their use of words is exercised 90 to 95 percent more than their use of images and so it takes awhile for them to draw with as much ease as they write.

Children are inspired by my enthusiasm for this kind of response, this kind of participation in their religion classes and perhaps this accounts for their success as religious artists. I absolutely believe in what Aristotle, the philosopher, observed: "The soul never thinks without an image."

Things to Think About

1. What personal experience have you had of drawing as an expression of prayer?

2. What might be some values of drawing prayers?

3. What has been the reaction of your students when you had them draw their prayers?

Things to Do

1. Find some quiet time and a comfortable place. Have at hand some blank paper and a box of crayons, marking pens or paints. Place yourself in God's presence. Let your mind and heart play in terms of what you feel like communicating to God. It might be gratitude for so many good things in your life. It might be a sense of confusion or doubt about what is happening in your life. It might be praise at God's greatness and goodness, or sorrow for something you have done, or petition for something you need or want. Relax and let your prayer express itself through your drawing materials. When you finish, enjoy and study what you have drawn or painted. Hang it in your room at home as a visual stimulus for prayer.

2. For an appropriate lesson introduce the children to drawing their prayers. Suggest, for example, that they identify with one of the persons in a gospel story, like a blind man who hears that Jesus is coming, or who has just been cured by Jesus. Ask them to draw the prayer that would rise up in their hearts if they were that person at that moment. When they have finished, encourage them to share what they have drawn.

22
Art and Photos

My first dealings with Carl were while he was teaching a fourth grade CCD class at St. Anthony's Parish near Catholic University in Washington, DC. He had never taught children before and was having numerous problems, one of which was getting them to pay attention to what he wanted them to learn. He quickly discovered that the lecture method didn't work. In desperation, he asked for help. One of 13 things I suggested was that he might use an art masterpiece of the story, "Jesus Calming the Storm," which was the biblical story in his next lesson. He used a large print of El Greco's painting from the National Gallery of Art and, to his amazement, it worked. The children liked looking at the story and talking about it from what they could see. Seemingly seeing Jesus calm the storm brought a level of calm to them. Many of the children had not been exposed to much sacred art, so the masterpiece was something different and fascinating. They found it attractive and appealing.

I have always used art, both sacred and secular, in my religion and other classes. It had been a strong and significant part of my childhood learning experiences in a one room schoolhouse in rural Iowa. Since my learning preference is visual, the value of seeing as part of the learning process had become ingrained. Art masterpieces as well as other kinds of pictures have always been a strong component in the curricula Carl and I have authored.

There are important reasons, beside my own personal ones, for using religious or sacred art in religion classes. Primary among these is that good art nurtures the inner eye, the eye of the soul, and when the inner eye is nurtured, holiness grows. Art, and photos, too, are helpful catalysts for prayer.

Many Cultures, Many Tastes

Let's reflect for a few moments on some of the potential for religious learning and prayer that the use of sacred art provides.

Often more than one painting of the face of Jesus, Mary, other biblical people or a biblical event or story is available. The variety reflects different countries, different cultures and different historical periods. This diversity reflects without words something of the length and breadth of the Catholic Christian experience.

Children, like adults, have different tastes. Using more than one artist's depiction allows for these differences. Also, the perception of a face, an event or a story that different artists have portrayed will bring into play a variety of aspects and nuances. Even the color choices made by artists will give unique messages to the viewers. An artist's bias may be revealed. His or her culture will be recognized in facial features, clothing, background. Masterpieces by artists from different countries can reveal to students the universality of Jesus, Mary and the scriptural events.

Long Tradition of Art in Prayer

In the early Christian catacombs, the massive Byzantine basilicas, the soaring cathedrals of Medieval Europe and the less imposing churches of today, pictures tell the story of Christianity and support the prayer of millions of believers. The story is passed on through unbelievably beautiful, carefully and lovingly designed awe-inspiring pictures, paintings, mosaics, icons, sculptures and colored glass. Except for a couple of intensely iconoclastic periods and communities, Christianity has from its earliest days appreciated the role of beauty, of art, in its teaching and worship.

Something deeply beautiful, as many art pieces are, has the power to impress the inner memory and leave traces of the person or the event on the soul. It also stirs a response that may easily become a prayer. This is so apparent in adult Catholics who, when they were children, were taught religion using the flipcharts with colored pictures made popular in the '30s, '40s and '50s by Father Aloysius Heeg, S.J. These were used in almost every parish and parochial school in the United States. In workshops Carl often shows one or more of these—especially the picture of the Guardian Angel and the Good Shepherd— and there is always an immediate and electrical response in the audience. These are certainly not great pieces of sacred art but even these locked themselves in the inner spirit's memory.

Wholistic Impact

Still another reason for using sacred art, especially of biblical events, is that they make it possible for children to take in the whole story at once. Although children tend to listen to a story as words unfold it, they sometimes become distracted before the end of the story is reached. This rarely happens when art is used rather than words. A good work of art communicates quickly and involves the feelings of the viewer immediately.

And still another reason is that children whose learning preference is visual will get so much more out of the classes in which art masterpieces and other pictures are used.

One more but certainly not the final reason for using art masterpieces and other religious art is that looking at and studying a piece often creates stillness in the group as well as in each individual child. I believe that these are gracious moments in which the Spirit's movement is felt, the Spirit's voice is heard and a communion with God occurs. They are moments of prayer. When this happens, no matter how briefly, transformation takes place, a child's faith is deepened, and catechesis becomes a change agent.

Photos

Photos are another primary tool in the art of teaching religion. The best are on a par with good art, and what they do to children is both similar and different.

An art masterpiece of Jesus, Mary or a biblical event shows children something or someone they haven't seen, whereas most photos show current events, contemporary people and familiar scenes or ones they can imagine in their worlds. One of the purposes of photos in religious education is to connect the story of God with the everyday story of humanity. God lives in our world and is revealed through its people, its things and its events. I believe deeply that if children are not helped to see and know God in everyday life, God will always be out of their reach. God will always be finding the child but the child won't really be caught. Or, it can be like children playing hide and seek with God. God does the hiding but the children don't have the clues to discover where God is.

Photos can't picture God, Jesus, Mary and other biblical characters because there are none available. However, photos of people who radically responded to God's call and were exemplary followers of Jesus can be used in religion classes to acquaint children with their stories and to inspire them to live faithfully, even heroically.

Photos can help children to appreciate God's created world as well as the great things that have been done in and to the world by people. They can also be used to help children see the bad things that have happened in and to the world because of people's lack of care. Photos can also open children to prayers of praise and thanks to God for people and things, to prayers of sorrow for what is bad and to prayers of petition for help to overcome the evils that are portrayed.

Photos are also useful in helping children make associations. Here is an example of a lesson drawing heavily on photos.

In teaching children that there is sin in the world but that God forgives sinners, the class might begin by studying photos or photo-like art that show people doing hurtful and wrong things.

Then they might hear or read the gospel story of Zacchaeus who was a sinner and is completely and lovingly forgiven by Jesus.

Finally, they can learn through photos and words that Jesus, through the priest, forgives in the sacrament of reconciliation or the act of a parent forgiving a child, a child forgiving a parent, a friend forgiving a friend.

Photos are good for evoking responses—What is a person in the photo doing? How does the action affect someone else in the photo? Or, what might the person or people in the photo do next? How do you feel about what you see happening in the photo? What do you know about yourself that would make you sure that you wouldn't act that way? What do you know about yourself that tells you that you would act as lovingly, as helpfully, as honestly? Or, tell a pretend or real story about a time when you or someone else did something or didn't do something like the people in the photo are doing. The suggestive quality of photos—and of art as well—makes visual images especially useful for creating a sense of sharing and community among the children.

Photos are powerful insofar as they initiate dialogue within the heart as well as the mind's eye and that kind of dialogue often is or leads to a prayerful response. Photos used in a religious context such as a religion class are ultimately vehicles to encourage children to look more and more at life with a religious or a faith perspective and respond prayerfully out of that perspective.

Meditating, Contemplating

Photos, secular and sacred art are very useful for focusing children for meditation or contemplation. I like to display a carefully selected photo or artwork before the children arrive for class. Sometimes I place it so they will see it right away, at other times I place it in our prayer corner.

At the appropriate moment in the lesson I ask the children to come closer around the picture and to become very still. I tell them to take a few minutes to look at the picture and think about the feelings or ideas it stirs in them. I suggest that they talk silently to God

about what they see and feel and I remind them of God's presence with them as they look at the picture.

I have found it takes a little practice for children to become comfortable with this kind of meditating or contemplating because they are so used to moving quickly from picture to picture in magazines and on TV. They are not used to stopping and gazing at a visual image with a certain sense of expectation and openness.

Making Up Prayers

Another prayer technique I have used with children and pictures, both photos and art, is to have them look closely at the image and then to pray aloud spontaneously whatever sentiments the picture stirs in their hearts. Or I ask them to write a prayer suggested by the picture. If there are a number of pictures, such as when the students tear out photos from magazines and newspapers, the children can make up a litany of prayers expressive of what the several visual images stir in them.

Slide-Sound Prayers

Carl has taken an interesting, slightly modernized, version of Gounod's *Ave Maria* and put it together with selected pieces of art showing Mary at various moments of her life from the annunciation to her assumption and glorification. It makes a beautiful prayer experience because the combination of art and music does much more than can one or the other alone.

Carl has created similar slide-sound prayers using Joe Wise's song, "Lord, Teach Me to Pray," John Fischer's "Jesus My Lord" and Deanna Edward's "My Road." We used the latter as part of confirmation preparation at Good Shepherd Parish in Alexandria, Virginia. At the start of the weeks of preparation we played "My Road" for the students and their catechists with Carl's photos as a final prayer experience during that evening. Then during the weeks of preparation one of the parishioners took close-up shots of each of the youngsters at various moments as they were caught up in different class experiences. He then put the best of the slides with several of Carl's more symbolic slides and Deanna Edward's song. The evening before the Confirmation ceremony, as part of the final stage of preparation, the students, their parents and the catechists looked and listened to the slide-song show. Hardly a parent's eye was dry by the end of the song, "My Road," illustrated with their children's photos.

Some Helpful Hints

Some hints for using art and photos effectively and affectively for learning and for prayer in religion classes are:

• To the extent possible, use good art and good photos. Always be on the lookout for ones that inspire you. As often as I can when I'm on vacation or doing other kinds of travel, I try to visit the local fine art gallery and look for a masterpiece or photo that might be used in my religion classes. Because I sometimes give each child a postcard size copy of a masterpiece, I collect these also. *Magazines, Papers, Books.*

• At times have the masterpiece or photo dsplayed on an art easel or on a wall in a prominent place in the room where you are teaching and gather around it for study and/or prayer during the moments it will be used in class.

Be consistent in your style of bringing children into communion with a piece of art or a photo. For example, always ask them to look at it in silence and while they are looking at it to ask themselves three questions:

—What do I see?

—What do I feel?

—What do I like?

While looking invite them to quietly ask the Holy Spirit to help them to see deeply into the picture.

Secondly, have them share what they see, what they feel, what they like.

Thirdly, point out some things that you consider significant, such as color, line, artist, historical period, culture and other things that you may know about the selection.

Next ask questions about the story it tells or the person it portrays in relation to the overall message of the lesson.

Finally, give each one a postcard size copy of it to add to their personal collection, especially if you started building one at the beginning of the year.

• At times take field trips. For example, I have taken classes to see an original such as "The Last Supper" by Salvador Dali at the National Gallery of Art in Washington, DC. This requires preparation beforehand and afterward, over and above the details of permission slips, transportation and help on the part of parents who accompany and assist.

The preparation that I do beforehand is to tell the children what masterpiece we will be looking at, some background on the artist, the country of origin, the historical period and the artist's style.

Sometimes I make up a card listing things they are to look for in the painting and as they see to check each one off.

As always they ponder the questions:

—What do I see?

—What do I feel?

—What do I like?

They are also urged to pray to the Holy Spirit for help in seeing more.

While at the gallery I tell the children as much as I have learned about the painting, or a guide who has agreed to be with us talks to the children about it.

Afterward we share as much as possible about the painting and sometimes we make our own masterpieces, in this instance, of the "Last Supper."

After a field trip, if a postcard size is available, I always give each one a personal copy.

As with the images that children draw, art and photos add to their soul's language and enrich their spirits and their lives. I fully believe what Cyril of Jerusalem, an early church father, observed: "Faith by seeing is stronger than faith by hearing."

Things to Think About

1. What has been your experience of art and photos as helps to your prayer?

2. What are some of the photos and art pieces that have most moved you to pray?

3. What success or problems have you had using visual images in your religion classes both for instruction and for prayer?

Things to Do

1. Try meditating with a strong photo or work of art. Find a quiet time and place. Display the picture in a way that allows you to look at it comfortably. Allow a moment or two to relax and quiet yourself. Recall that God is present with you and the Holy Spirit prays within you. Then gaze at the picture for a few moments. Don't worry about detail at first. Allow the visual to resonate within you. Note ideas or feelings that rise up inside you. Express silently in your heart any prayers that surface. Then gradually glance at details in the picture, noticing what they suggest, how they make you feel. Through all this simply pray as the picture and the Spirit move you. At the end you might like to write a brief prayer summing up the experience.

2. To find photos and art that you find helpful for prayer get in the habit of hanging up in your home or apartment one or more that speak to you. Let them move you to pray when you glance at them. After a week, replace one with a photo or art work that you now find more prayerful and moving. In this way you develop from experience your own taste for prayerful pictures. Then keep the better ones in a file or drawer for use during classes.

3. Have the children build a collection of pictures that are good "prayer-starters." They can find them in magazines and newspapers, in books and museums, perhaps among photos they, their family or friends have taken on vacation. Give children an opportunity to put good slides with a popular song that they find meaningful. Use it for prayer in an upcoming class.

23
Music and Song

I am always fascinated when I hear someone repeat Augustine's statement that "the person who sings, prays twice." And, even though my imagination doesn't help me in discerning all that the saying means, I believe that it is true. Growing up in rural Iowa as a child and a teenager, I remember vividly St. Peter's Church in Temple Hill and St. Mary's in Cascade resounding with the whole congregation singing hymns like "Tantum Ergo" and "Holy God, We Praise Thy Name." It seemed to me then as it does now that when we sang we prayed our hearts out.

Presently Carl and I are parishioners at Holy Trinity Parish in Washington, DC, and the singing of hymns in our congregation is as enthusiastic and wholehearted. Both my past and present experience suggest that when people gather to pray, especially liturgically and paraliturgically, it is necessary to break into song. Music transforms what we want to say to God. Music enriches and enhances our personal and communal response to God's initiation of prayer in us. Music is like an elevator in the act of lifting our minds and hearts to God.

I realized the power of song and music in a poignant way when my sister, Janet, was dying of cancer. Near the end, her pain and her sadness about leaving her husband and two children were almost more than she could bear. Father White, their pastor, sensing Janet's feelings, dropped by one morning with a bag of donuts. He said he would share his donuts if she would share her coffee. Laughing, Janet invited him in and, as they ate, told him that when she tried to rest, her anxieties about death increased and that she grew sadder about leaving Rich, Brett and Jenny.

Father White had come prepared and he gave Janet a couple cassettes of prayerful songs by the St. Louis Jesuits. He told her to play them when she lay down to rest and just to listen quietly. Janet found that the music and the prayerful lyrics helped take her mind off her pain and worries. She found herself praying along with the lyrics of the songs and relaxing until she would finally doze off.

147

Father White shared coffee and donuts with Janet often during her last months and he continued to supply her with tapes of prayerful songs that helped her find peace, to accept death and the awful separation from her beloved family.

Her experience convinced me, in a profound way, of the prayer-power of music and song.

Music and Catechists

What does this mean for us who are responsible for bringing up a new generation of pray-ers? I believe it means that we build music and song into the catechetical moments as well as into the liturgical and paraliturgical ones. The question, "What do you do if you don't sing well or do not play a musical instrument?" often comes up. I suffer from a lack in both of those areas so I have had to find ways to sing and use music without a good voice and without being able to accompany the children with an instrument. I am able to lead the children in simple songs like "Kum Bah Yah" and "Silent Night" and in hymns that I have sung many, many times. For most of the music and song, though, I use a record or a cassette player. Fortunately, for me and other non-musicians, most catechetical programs (such as *This Is Our Faith* published by Silver Burdett & Ginn) have a song and music program. Components to those programs are records and cassettes for each grade level and manuals with many suggestions for using the music and songs easily and well. Some of the music is for listening and meditative prayer, others are songs of praise and thanksgiving, and others capture the spirit and meaning of the lessons.

Music and the Young

The power of music in children and young people today is evidenced by the listening that they do for hours at a time through headsets and stereo equipment. Allan Bloom, a professor of social thought at the University of Chicago, began an article in *The Washington Post* with the paragraph, "Nothing is more singular about this generation of students than its addiction to music. To find a rival to this enthusiasm, one would have to go back at least a century to Germany and the passion for Wagner's operas. They had the religious sense that Wagner was creating the meaning of life and that they were not merely listening to his works but experiencing that meaning."

I recognized for some years that music, mostly rock, made up the common environment or atmosphere or language shared by most teenagers. But only recently have I become more aware of how much younger children are at home with that same music. I noticed last year that our goddaughter, Angela, then in third grade, could sing along with many of the rock songs on the radio or TV. Then I began asking her for suggestions of hit songs that Carl and I might use in our religion classes. She recommended several with hardly a moment's hesitation. She loved Whitney Houston's songs most of all. Her third-grade friends not only liked the same music, but they all knew an amazing amount about the different rock stars and groups.

Using music and song in religion classes is maximizing on this passion in our children and young people. And the possibilities are almost endless.

I have recently begun using popular music, which today means, for the most part, rock. Neither Carl nor I are particularly knowledgeable in the area of rock music. We are not able to keep up with the current hits, which change so rapidly. But, knowing how much this music means in the lives of most of our students, we have used a rock song in many of our junior high classes, and occasionally with fourth and sixth graders.

To find appropriate songs we rely largely on the newsletter *Top Music Countdown* (Tabor Publications) by Father Don Kimball, a disc-jockey on the West Coast, who strongly encourages the use of rock music as a powerful way to communicate with our young people. Each issue presents 25 current hit songs with suggestions as to how they each might be used in religion classes, liturgy and retreat experiences. We have also relied on the suggestions of our students and on helpful record store salespeople.

Some of the selections we have used successfully are "Kyrie" by Mr. Mister, "On the Road to Find Out" by Cat Stevens, Michael Jackson's "Man in the Mirror," "Faith" by George Michael, "Honestly" by Stryper, Sting's "If You Love Somebody," Bon Jovi's "Livin' on a Prayer," "Love of Another Kind" by Amy Grant, and Whitney Houston's "The Greatest Love of All." We have found that the songs speak to the students in a way few other media do, and our respectful use of music that they like seems to foster in them respect for us and for what we feel to be important.

Songs as Catalysts

Songs can be used to prime the inner pump. For example, the children might listen to the song "All Good Gifts" from the *Godspell* soundtrack and then offer individual and communal thanks for all the good things in God's creation. I've also used Joe Wise's "I Believe Lord," after which the children wrote their own statements of beliefs, their creeds, before we began to study the Apostles' Creed.

The children can also take a melody of a popular song they know, and create a prayer of their own. No less a catechist than Cardinal Robert Bellarmine, whose catechism became the model of most catechisms since Reformation times, including the *Baltimore Catechism*, regularly took popular love songs and rewrote the lyrics as a prayer or doctrinal summary.

Here is an example of a class experience with third graders who did the same thing with a popular song. The lesson dealt with movement—running, playing, jumping, swimming, dancing—and of not being able to move—being held motionless by someone stronger, or being paralyzed—and the gospel story of Jesus healing a paralyzed man.

Near the end of the class the students made up this prayer song to the melody of "Michael, Row Your Boat Ashore":

> Jesus healed the paralyzed man, Alleluia.
> Jesus, thanks that I can move, Alleluia.

Songs for Meditative Background

Songs like "Abba Father" by Carey Landry and "Earthen Vessels" by John Foley can add to what happens as children sculpt with clay. What would ordinarily be an art activity becomes a prayerful one when songs like the ones named above are part of it.

Some selections of Gregorian Chant are particularly useful in adding a prayerful atmosphere to moments when the students are reading, writing or doing another creative activity.

Many children are imaginative in the drawing of prayer doodles as they listen to songs like "The Breastplate of St. Patrick," or "Livin' on a Prayer," by Bon Jovi. Listening to prayers that have been put to music can also make them easier to learn by heart.

Songs in Prayer Celebrations

Liturgical and paraliturgical celebrations are other times in which music and song are necessary ingredients. Patricia Mathson, in a recent book of prayer services for children (Ave Maria Press) writes in the introduction, "Music is a joyful experience for children and a wonderful way to praise God. Its common language serves to unite them in prayer."

Music and songs may be used in many ways in prayer celebrations. For example, prayers like the Our Father and Hail Mary can be sung, phrases of the psalms can be chanted or the beat and the words of some rock songs can be used for listening and meditation. There are beautiful recordings of prayers like the "Breastplate of St. Patrick" and Francis of Assisi's popular "Peace Prayer."

I also use hymns that the children may be familiar with from Sunday Mass in their parishes. Using hymns in both settings may help the children link what they do in religion class with what they do in church on Sunday.

I often use songs as opening and closing prayers. A song like "When the Saints Go Marchin' In" adds spirit and impetus to an entrance procession.

Echoing phrases of songs is another delightful way to sing songs back and forth with children. Singing songs with simple gestures is a way to increase the children's enjoyment and attention. And having them join hands and move in various ways while listening to and singing along can make praying with songs more memorable. Singing only the refrain while the leader sings the rest is still another way for children to pray with song.

A more demanding but very rewarding way of entering more fully into a prayer song is to create a song-slide presentation. The students can select slides they feel fit the words of the sung prayer. Doing this helps them relate the prayer-song with real life experiences visualized by the slides.

Bible Songs

Another rich resource of music and song for prayer is traditional gospel music. Carl and I recognized the value of such songs when we visited the Holy Land. Our group was ecumenical, including several ministers from the Christian Church. At each place we visited, they sang spontaneously and with great fervor a song based on the biblical account of what occurred at that place.

We similarly use such songs from time to time in class when we know a song that tells the bible story of a lesson. Sometimes we draw upon authentic gospel music, like Mahalia Jackson singing "Were You There When They Crucified My Lord?" At other times we use songs modern composers have written to tell a bible story, like Mary Lou Walker's "Good Samaritan" or Joe Wise's "Jesus Was Asleep at the Head of the Boat."

Such songs not only tell a bible story in a captivating way, but they invite the students to enter into the story and respond to God, to Jesus, with the people in the story. Gospel music is inherently prayerful.

There are many more ways to pray with song and music. It takes courage, a belief in its value and some imagination.

Some Helpful Hints

Four things that I do before using a song in religion class or in prayer celebrations are these:

- I get to know the song as well as I can: its tempo—when is it slow, when is it fast; when should it be loud and soft; how many verses are there; does it have a refrain, a chorus? Is it a story song, a meditative one, a song that will lend itself easily to gestures and movement; a song that I like and which I feel my students will enjoy? What does the song say to me? How does it make me feel?

- The next thing that I do is determine how I will teach it. Rarely do I just say that we're going to sing a song and proceed to play it on the record player or cassette inviting them to listen to it first. No, I do everything I can to get them interested in it, to be open to it. I tell them what the song is about, why it is a good one for this lesson or celebration and teach it to them in small sections. Because I neither play a musical instrument nor sing easily and well, I go over the words of the song, clapping it with them in rhythm, until there is a familiarity with the words, the feeling, the thoughts reflected in the lyrics and the gestures and/ or movement if the latter is going to be part of the singing/praying experience.

- When I feel that we are ready to sing, we listen to it once softly. The children listen to it more carefully when it is played with as little volume as possible. Depending on the difficulty of the song, we may go over some of the words and the refrain. With rock songs whose lyrics are sometimes very difficult to make out, I provide the students with a copy of the lyrics. Sometimes they are hard to find, but many record albums have the lyrics printed on the outside. I ask the students to follow the words as they listen to the song, circling or underlining any words or phrases that particularly speak to them.

In instances where I know that the song may require listening to more than once before it can be sung easily and well, I have had a local musician do the song on a tape two or three times. I have found a real willingness in musicians to do this for me, especially the ones who are the school's music teachers. I have also found incredible generosity in local people who sing well and who like to do things that will enhance the lives of children.

- I am careful not to make the preparation for a song too long and too laborious. I do some of the same things in the same way every time we are going to sing a new song and the children become used to the pattern and enter into it cooperatively. I also repeat songs that the children and I like a lot because the effect of those songs transcends the words— bonding, delighting, enabling every child to participate in what's going on, providing a vehicle for releasing feelings. Music instructs on every level of the human spirit and it makes it possible, as the saying goes, "to pray twice."

Things to Think About

1. What has been your personal experience of music and song as a help to or an expression of prayer? Do you "pray twice" when you sing?

2. How do you feel about singing in church? Does it help you pray? Does it help you feel more a part of a worshipping community? Does it appear more a distraction, keeping you from prayer?

3. What do you feel about the music most young people seem addicted to? How do you feel about using rock music in your religion classes?

Things to Do

1. If you are not familiar with some of the better rock songs, find someone who is more knowledgeable—your own children or your students or a young person working in a record store or Father Kimball's newsletter—to suggest one or two songs that would be good for prayer and for religion class. Find a time when you will not be disturbed. Listen to a song several times. If you cannot make out the words, look up the lyrics. Be as open and receptive as you can. Focus on its main message, its repeated images or words, its beat. Then evaluate the experience. You may or may not like the song. It may or may not suit your taste. But write down what you feel it is saying and reflect on how its message fits with the gospels and what you are teaching.

2. If your religion program has a music component, select a song on the record or cassette available for the grade you are teaching. Make up gestures to use with the children as you are singing and praying the song together.

3. Be alert to hymns and songs that are frequently and enthusiastically sung during Masses in your parish. Use them occasionally in your religion classes.

24
Story and Poetry

Story and poetry are particularly valuable resources for helping children to pray and to learn what prayer is.

Both story and poetry have special power to penetrate life's mysteries where prayer finds its spark and fuel. Good stories and poems take children beyond the ordinary, the ho-hum, the pedestrian. Through them their imaginations are sparked, their affections are engaged and their view of life is greatly expanded. This makes them helpful prayer resources.

Poetry: Some Examples

Here is a poem I wrote and titled, "I Wonder If the Gift of Me."

I watched you
As you watched us play.
I saw you by yourself today.
I wonder if the gift of ME. . . .
Would set the LONELY in you free?

The poem reveals the empty, gnawing pain of loneliness that many children experience, while suggesting that its cure lies not in accumulating or receiving things but in the gift of personal, caring presence. Without moralizing, I simply read the poem to the children and give them time to reflect on and respond to it.

I might ask a question or two like: When have you felt like the lonely person in the poem? When have you seen someone like her and wondered what you could do to help? Or I might have them draw a situation in which they felt like the lonely child, or reached out to help a lonely person.

153

Their reflection and/or creative response leads easily into prayer of various kinds, like composing a prayer for lonely people, a prayer to know best how to respond to people who are lonely, a litany for lonely people they know.

A poem can also be used prayerfully to help ease the transition of a new child into a new home, a new school, a new neighborhood. And, also, to inspire the "old" children to be sensitive, caring and open to the newcomer. For that particular situation I wrote the poem "Together."

> I knocked upon your new front door.
> I asked if you were in.
> I wanted you to know next door
> There's someone for a friend.
> There's someone you can be with
>   if you miss the friends you had.
> There's nothing like TOGETHER
> To turn sad into glad.

After reading the poem, I might ask questions like, Have you ever done anything like the child in the poem is doing? Or, have you ever wished someone would have done that for you? What is it like to miss friends? What do the two lines "There's nothing like TO-GETHER / To turn sad into glad" mean to you?

Then I might introduce the new child and ask her to tell us where he or she lived before, and where she lives now.

I might ask who, in the class, lives nearby.

We might listen to "The Visit," a song on Joe Wise's record, *Close Your Eyes.*

We might join hands and pray together a litany with invocations and responses made up by the children or myself. For example:

> For Susan who has moved here from Chicago. . . .
>   Help us to make her feel welcome, Lord.
> Because it is good to have Susan with us. . . .
>   We thank you, Lord.
> For all of us here TOGETHER. . . .
>   We praise you, O Lord.

With young children I might read *Sometimes I Get Lonely—Psalm 42 For Children* by Elspeth Campbell Murphy, as a closing prayer.

I might have the Argus poster that says, "There is no place that Jesus is not" on a stand or on a wall nearby just for the children to see and take in on their own.

A caution: Should you be in a school where new students might be homeless and coming to school from a shelter, I would not recommend this poem or this prayer experience. I would, however, do whatever I could personally to make sure the child feels welcome and precious.

There are many other wonderful poems that might be used for prayer. See the Bibliography at the end of this book.

A Helpful Pattern

The key to using story and poetry as helps to praying and to reveal prayer's varied ways is to allow the children and the story or poem to interact without interference or moralization on your part. The story or poem can enable the children to perceive in a fresh way what they have already experienced. They can then be encouraged to articulate their responses in prayer.

I usually follow the simple pattern suggested above. I vary it as circumstances differ. To exemplify the pattern more explicitly I'll share how I use a marvelous piece of children's literature, *Yussel's Prayer*, by Barbara Cohen.

Prepare for the story or poem.   I do this initial step for several reasons. Sometimes there is information needed. For example, *Yussel's Prayer* centers on the Yom Kippur celebration. So before we read the story, I explore with the children their knowledge of this important Jewish holy day. Many of the children or their familiies may have Jewish friends from whom they have garnered some knowledge of Yom Kippur. I've found that a worksheet asking them to write everything they know about the Jewish people and Yom Kippur to be helpful in drawing out their knowledge of the feast. I supplement their knowledge with further information that I feel will help make Yussel's story more accessible to them.

At other times the preparation focuses on the children's experience or present knowledge of a reality explored in a story or poem. For example, if I am using *Yussel's Prayer* in a lesson specifically on prayer, I might prepare by asking the children to write or draw what they mean by prayer, or to share some of their prayer experiences. In this way the children may be more ready to relate Yussel's experience to their own.

Experience the story or poem.   I read the story or poem to the children as they listen, or I read the story and show slides of its illustrations at the same time so they can see the illustrations as well as hear the story. I make every effort to let the children see the illustrations as they listen to the words. I usually sit with the children gathered around me in such a way that I can read the book upside down so they can see the illustrations. This takes some practice but is very workable. You may prefer reading the story only and letting the children illustrate it out of their imaginations.

Respond reflectively to the story or poem.   It is important that the children have a chance to interact with the poem or story. I normally encourage a period of reflection, either in silence, with individuals thinking about the story or poem with questions I suggest, or through sharing their responses. The sharing may simply be responding aloud to my questions, writing, drawing or otherwise expressing their responses in creative ways. Some stories or poems may suggest action responses, such as a decision to pray more or in a new way.

From *Yussel's Prayer* children learn things about prayer that they may not have thought much about before, for example:

- Prayer that doesn't come from the heart may never reach heaven.
- Prayer doesn't have to be formal; it doesn't have to be a specific set of words; it doesn't have to use any words at all.

• God listens to the prayer of anyone—uneducated as well as educated, young as well as old, out in the pasture as well as in a temple, synagogue, or church.

Prayer sparked by the poem or story.   To move now to praying seems a natural step. I usually invite the children to pray in ways that flow out of their interaction with the story or poem. For example, in relation to the story about Yussel, the children work in pairs. Together each pair is challenged to create a prayer that they feel the gates of heaven would open wide to let in. They write and read them or pray them with gesture and movement or sing them or play them on an instrument. We have, on occasion, written them up descriptively, put them into a booklet and used them for prayer during succeeding classes.

Stories: Some Examples

Here are several more examples that may suggest the rich prayer potential of stories and poems. I use these within the above process, but will here simply suggest the literary piece and its use for praying.

The Legend of the Blue Bonnet, a beautiful story retold by Tomie dePaola, is about an Indian girl who sacrifices her most valuable possession, a doll made for her by her mother, to help bring rain to her drought-stricken people. The children dramatized the story as part of the Liturgy of the Word in the parish Sunday Eucharist. It was a powerful prayer experience for young and old alike.

Margaret Wise Brown's *The Runaway Bunny* is an exquisite story about a mother rabbit telling how she will pursue her little bunny who keeps threatening to run away. It suggests in a deep and believable way the constant, pursuing presence of a loving God. I often use it in relation to Psalm 139, which describes God's presence with us no matter where we may go. The version of the psalm that I use with younger children is Mary Elspeth Campbell's *Where Are You God?*

I use Robert Munsch's *Love You Forever* in a similar way with texts like Isaiah 54:8-10, Jeremiah 31:3, Hosea 11:1-9. The story tells of a mother's unchanging love for her son, from birth through childhood, adolescence and young manhood, until she dies and he continues the same changeless and unconditional love for his own infant daughter. After enjoying the story and exploring the biblical texts the children pray, for example by writing a prayer to God expressing how they feel being so loved by God.

Another example of relating a piece of children's literature with a biblical passage and leading to prayer is my use of M.B. Goffstein's *An Artist.* I first ask the children to draw a picture or create something from clay or aluminum foil. Then I read this brief, delightful story of an artist. The story suggests the creation stories of Genesis and tells the children in an exquisite way that an artist is like God and affirms their likeness to God in what they have just done as "artists" themselves. Following the story we thank God for being able to use crayons, paints, brushes, paper, clay or aluminum foil to say important and beautiful things.

I find a story like Claudia Fregosi's *A Gift* most helpful for introducing the children into the meaning of sacramental, liturgical prayer. This Indian tale tells of a husband's efforts to reveal his love for his wife through several gifts he makes for her—a pair of slippers, a necklace, a bracelet and finally a blanket in which she may wrap herself. After hearing the story and reflecting on it, it is natural to pray a prayer of thanks to God for many gifts of love. One I like is a Byzantine liturgical prayer of thanksgiving that sums up the whole sacramental experience.

> For the favor of being, we thank You, Lord;
>   for the Father, who Is, we praise You!
> For the truth of our faith, we thank You, Lord;
>   for the Word, who is Truth, we praise You!
> For the gift of our love, we thank You, Lord;
>   for the Gift who is Love, we praise You!
> For the love of our mother, we thank You, Lord;
>   for your Mother in heaven, we praise You!
> For the work of our father, we thank You, Lord;
>   for the Work of your Hand, we praise You! . . .
> For the joys of the earth, we thank You, Lord;
>   for your Heavenly Joy we praise You!
> For bread and for wine, we thank You, Lord;
>   for your Body and Blood, we praise You!
> For the lightness of air, we thank You, Lord;
>   for your Creating Breath, we praise You!
> For the coolness of water, we thank You, Lord;
>   for your Waters of Mercy, we praise You!
> For the passing of time, we thank You, Lord;
>   for your Endless Duration, we praise You! . . . .
> For the sorrows of humans, we thank you, Lord;
>   for your Passion on Earth, we praise You!
> For the coming of death, we thank You, Lord;
>   for your Death on the Cross, we praise You!
> For the splendors of life, we thank You, Lord;
>   for your Rising in Splendor, we praise You!
> For the host of your saints, we thank You, Lord;
>   for Yourself, who are Holy, we praise You!
> Give thanks to the Lord, O you his children,
>   for the Lord is your Life
>   and the Lord is your Love,
> And blessed are those who live and who love!
> Give praise to the Lord for his promise
>   of everlasting joy! Amen.

Another use of story introduces children to the wonderful reality that prayer is something that most people do, something that goes on all over the world. A good book for this is Byrd Baylor's *The Way to Start a Day*.

Many, many stories and poems written for children can be used to inspire and to connect them with the mystery of God and of life and to deepen their awareness of people and situations that might be helped by prayer. Those mentioned above and several that I have used successfully are listed in the Bibliography at the end of this book. You might start with these, adapt the process I sketched above, and explore further on your own the marvellous prayer potential of story and poetry.

Stories Children Write

Children are also capable of writing stories that touch on life's mysteries and thereby lend themselves to reflection and prayer. Here is one written by our nine-year-old god-child, Angela, in her fourth grade religion class.

Angela
Barbieri
Age 9

I have a friend named Ana. I also have another friend named Kate. Yesterday I went to Ana's house and she started saying mean things about Kate. I didn't like that but I never told Ana. I also didn't tell Kate because she is my friend and I don't like it when people hurt her feelings. I don't like it when anybody hurts some-body's feelings. Kate and Ana are both great friends for me!!

After reading her story and encouraging Angela to comment further on it, here is how I might use it to move the class into prayer.

I have used a story like Angela's in prayer celebrations about friendship. A particularly good liturgical celebration on "Friends," one that I have used several times, is in *Liturgies for Little Ones* by Carol Rezy (Ave Maria Press).

Angela's story might be read to open or to introduce the theme. In Carol Rezy's celebration the first reading is a paraphrase of Sirach 6:14-17:

> A faithful friend is a sure shelter. Whoever finds one has found a real treasure. A faithful friend is something beyond price. You cannot measure his worth. Those who love the Lord will find real friends.

It is a near perfect biblical reading for a prayer experience on friendship.

The petitions can reflect the children's need for help in being faithful and good friends.

Songs that are about friendship can be sung. One that I have used a lot and which young children, fourth grade and under, really get into is "Open the Circle," by Jack Miffleton, on his record *Holy House.* The song begins:

> Open the circle for Mia,
> Welcome, welcome in!
> Open the circle for Mia,
> She's a very good friend.

There are more lines, and then the children name others they want to welcome in and the song repeats until all the children in the group are named.

Things to Think About

1. What has been your own experience of prayer related to poetry and stories?

2. Why do you feel stories and poems are such special resources for helping children pray and learn more about prayer?

3. What hesitations do you have in building stories and poems into your religion classes?

4. What resources are available to you for finding good stories and poems for your classes?

Things to Do

1. Select an appropriate lesson in which you could use one of the examples sketched out above. Follow the process, adapting it to your own situation as needed. Then evaluate how it went.

2. To deepen your conviction about the importance of story and poetry in religious education and prayer, read a good book on the value of literature in relation to faith and prayer. (See the Bibliography at the end of this book.)

3. Consult your local librarian or a book about children's books and poems. Select one. Read it. Let it speak to you. Respond to it prayerfully in your own way. Try another book or poem. After experiencing the power of poetry and story for prayer yourself, you may feel more confident in using them with your students.

25
Movement, Gesture and Dance

Children and movement are almost synonymous. If you're a "child-watcher" as I am, you know how hard it is for them to sit or stand still very long at a time. For most children, to be alive is to be on the move.

This desire, this need in children to move can be an asset in our religion classes, especially during prayer times.

Instead of having the children sit at their desks while praying, invite them to move to another area of the room that has been set up as a prayer place, a prayer corner, a prayer square or circle.

For example, I teach my once-a-week religion class in the library of St. Luke's School in McLean, Virginia. There are enough chairs and space to make a prayer circle. I could make better use of this than I do but on the occasions when we have moved to the prayer circle and prayed it has been a memorable experience. It is not just the movement to the place for prayer, we also use our bodies to pray. For example, after gathering in the circle we might take the Bible in our hands, open it and then lift it upward while praying a phrase from the psalms such as, "Your word, O Lord, is a light to guide me" (based on Psalm 119:105). Or we sing a prayer while shaking cymbals and maracas, jingling bells, thumping on a drum and clapping our hands. Or we stand and do simple gestures that express the sentiments of the prayer.

Kathryn Fredgren, a professional dancer and the owner-director with her husband, Ken, of the Arlington Center For Dance, says the importance of gesture and movement in prayer arises out of the truth that we don't just go to God with our minds, we need to pray with our whole selves.

Jack Miffleton, Carey Landry, Carol Jean Kinghorn, Nancy Quinn and others who

161

have composed lyrics, music and related religion materials for children frequently suggest gestures to go with their musical scores.

The ancient song "Lord of The Dance," in which Jesus dances out his life, suggests that in dance, new life takes shape; in dance, the spirit is enlivened; in dance, deep and lasting joy can be experienced; in dance, prayer is done and not just said.

In the scriptures we read of David dancing before the Ark of the Lord (2 Sm 6:14-15). In the psalms there are verses like "Let them praise his name in the festive dance" (Ps 149:3). St. Jerome, the translator of the Bible, wrote: "The joy of the Spirit finds expression in bodily gesture."

If all this is true, then it also has to be true that catechesis and worship are impoverished to the extent that the body is not more consciously involved.

I had taught religion for many years before I felt comfortable praying with gestures or doing simple liturgical dance with the children. My first attempts were done uneasily, clumsily and, at best, rigidly; the children responded uneasily, clumsily and rigidly. Some simply watched my pathetic efforts sympathetically or with a kind of respectful scorn. After several such experiences I gave up trying this type of prayer activity but I couldn't shake the feeling that movement, gesture and dance were necessary ingredients, even if they were limited.

Years went by, as I harbored this feeling, yet I did none of it in my religion classes other than making the Sign of the Cross, folding our hands, bowing our heads and genuflecting.

Learning to Move Prayerfully

Then one Sunday, in our parish bulletin, there was an announcement that Kathryn Fredgren was offering 12 consecutive classes in liturgical movement. I signed up for the course. For the first few weeks of classes my body was mostly out of step with my thoughts and feelings, but gradually it got more in step. Gradually, too, I lost a feeling of embarrassment as the smaller and simpler movements I was making became larger and more complicated. I began to tell stories through the expressions on my face and the controlled movements of my body.

The most memorable moment for me was a simple three-part interpretative gesture of reconciliation that another member of the class and I did for and with the class during a paraliturgy. As we stood estranged, back to back, another member of the class read a passage describing many things that separate us.

Following the reading I turned toward her and touched her on the shoulder, a silent outward gesture expressing a desire for forgiveness, a need for reconciliation. She reached up and placed her hand over mine. Then we turned joyously toward each other and lovingly embraced. How good it felt to be completely reconciled!

Yet how simple the movements and gestures. The power of interpretative gesture is awesome but this power is neither fully released nor experienced unless it is actively entered into. The bodily movements must flow from and deepen an inner feeling, idea or conviction. Children can do something as simple; so can adolescents and adults. Patience is needed and a care that body and spirit are honestly at one in the physical expression.

A Gesture and Movement Workshop

A couple of months later I shared in a workshop by Sister Micaela Randolph, a Benedictine from Atchison, Kansas, who had a lot of experience with children and dance. Her workshop was "The Body as a Vehicle of Prayer." Everything Micaela did with us was rooted in what she told us at the beginning of her session: "Prayer always begins with God. He speaks to us in a thousand different ways. His word evokes from us a response. That response can be expressed in many different ways. Let us learn to respond to God in a very beautiful, harmonious and unified way . . . that of dancing. . . ."

She had us do very simple things that we might readily do with our students—pretending that we had a butterfly in our hand and in slow motion letting go of it and then trying to catch it; resting on the floor pretending that the sun was beating down on us, then letting ourselves be drawn up into the sun trying to feel its warmth; writing the name Jesus in the air with large flowing motions; being given a line of poetry or prayer and interpreting it with our own gestures.

The most helpful and immensely practical thing that I learned from Sister Micaela is what she calls the "ABC of Movement" and describes as five basic movements from which our actions derive: *locomotion* (forward, backwards and sideways), *elevation* (up, down), *falling, turning around*, and *gesturing*.

During our workshop she tailored the five to four and told us to think in terms of going *up*, going *down*, *walking*, and *turning around*. Each of us took these and put them together into one flowing line of movement and showed it to the others. As I did this I felt I was dancing—simply, yes, but creatively because I spontaneously inserted rhythm; there was a shape to what I did and the flow of my movements took on its own dynamic. For the first time, I easily and freely moved away from my own space into "outer" space. This was all the motivation I needed to do something on my own.

Since that time I have used gesture, movement and dance easily and, most of the time, well in my religion classes. Perhaps it's because I do it with assured confidence, but I have also found children very responsive to this kind of praying. I don't pray with movement in every class but often. I have also encouraged children to create their own movements to phrases from the psalms, verses of songs, prayer responses and traditional prayers like the Our Father, the Glory Be or St. Francis' Canticle of the Sun.

Some of the ways that I have used gesture and movement are these:

• *Enthroning the Bible.*   This can be done in a variety of ways but the way I normally do it is through an enthronement ceremony, always during the first class. I have described this earlier in the chapter on the Bible, but it may bear repeating in this chapter.

I hold up the Bible, tell the children that it is the most important book that we have as Christians and that words from this great and special book will be read, talked about and prayed in every class. I try to impress upon them that the Book is holy and that we will always handle it with love and care. I tell them also that the Bible, God's Book, will have its own special place in our midst and that together we will put it there now. I ask for a volunteer to carry the Book and I show him or her how to carry it reverently. I also tell them that "God's word is a light to guide us," so we need another volunteer to carry a candle, sometimes lighted, sometimes not. Then starting from a place in the room farthest from the spot where the Bible will be enthroned, the rest of the children form either a single or double line. I show them how to walk so that their whole bodies reveal their respect and reverence for God's Book. I put on music with a beat but very softly, and together we carry the Bible and place it and the candle on the table or stand reserved for it. Then each of us bows to or kisses the Book and returns to our places.

• *Praying a litany.*   The words that are repeated following lines of a litany can be prayed in gesture as well as with words. If a litany is prayed while the children are standing in a circle and the response is something like, "We give you thanks with our whole selves, O Lord," the children might join hands and lift them slowly upward while praying the response and bring them slowly downward as a reflective pause before going on to the next invocation. If doing this, I recommend that the litany be no more than five invocations long.

• *Poems.*   Sometimes poems are prayers with movement words and expressions in them, for example this one that I made up and have used with children.

> The wind is skipping
>   through the leaves
> So happy on its way.
> The sun is like a
>   warming hug
> That brightens up our day.
> To thank you, God,
>   for these great gifts
> We lift our arms and pray.
>   Amen.

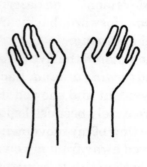

I have the children gather in a circle, join hands, skip to the right on the first eight syllables (the first two lines) and skip to the left on the second six syllables (the 3rd line). Stop and let go of hands. During the next eight syllables (the fourth, fifth and sixth lines) each one makes a large circular arc with his or her right hand and arm, bringing it full circle. Then with both arms folded over their chests, they hug themselves. On the next eight syllables (the seventh and eighth lines) they join hands again and walk rhythmically to the right. Stop and on the last line raise their arms upward, let go, hold for a moment, and bring them down slowly to a rest on "Amen."

• *Mirroring.*   I teach the children, through mirroring, the prayer and gestures for making the Sign of the Cross (many already know them, some do not). Mirroring is a very practical technique for teaching gestures. Make the sign of the cross for yourself as you look in a mirror. This is how you look to the children. When you touch your hand to your left shoulder it looks like your right shoulder. So, not to confuse the children, you demonstrate the gestures backwards. If you want them to touch their left shoulder, facing them you touch your right shoulder with your left hand. They will automatically touch their left shoulder!

I try to help them appreciate that the gesture is as important as the words to the prayer. Angela, our godchild, was so into the importance of the gestures, that when her mother inadvertently put her hand on Angela's right shoulder while she was making the Sign, Angela became upset and said, "Don't do that, Mom, you're breaking my Spirit."

• *Kiss of peace.* Another gesture that most children are familiar with is the handshake or kiss of peace during Mass. We talk about its significance as a gesture that brings us into brief communion with someone else who is part of our worshipping family. It is a gesture that says to another, "I wish you peace," "I wish you well," "I wish you God's blessings," "I acknowledge you as my sister or brother in Christ."

• *Psalms.* Creating gestures to express the meaning of verses of the psalms is another way that I frequently use movement prayerfully in my religion classes. For example Ps 8, Ps 9:1, Ps 13, Ps 139: 1-12, Ps 23, Ps 25:1.

• *Pantomiming.* Pantomiming phrases of prayers is another creative way to involve children in reflective and original movement. The children, in pairs or individually, study one of the phrases and try out movements until they are satisfied or ready. Then we gather in a circle and each pair or individual pantomimes the phrase assigned while the rest of us pray aloud the prayer from beginning to end. Sometimes, too, we learn the movements from each other and together pantomime and pray aloud the prayer.

• *Sculpting.* Giving the children opportunities to mold clay or aluminum foil while they are listening to music or a song is still another way that movement can be, at times, prayerfully part of the class.

Making a human sculpture can also be exciting. For example, ask the children what they mean by church or some other reality. Then invite one of the children to show his or her meaning of church just through bodily position. The next child then joins his meaning with the previous one, again by bodily position alone, but now in relation to the previous child. In this way they gradually build a "church" sculpture just through how their bodies express their ideas and feelings. For example, they might end up with a pyramid, or a circle, or a circle with an opening, or . . . . who knows?

• *Blessings.* One of the most touching and meaningful ways that I have involved children in prayerful gesture is through blessings. For example, the verse:

> Awake, O sleeper
> arise from the dead,
> and Christ will give you light (Eph 5:14).

The children put their heads on their desks and close their eyes, as though sleeping. They remain that way for a few moments. Then I gently touch each one on the head with the words, "Awake, O sleeper" while each child slowly awakens and lifts his or her head. Then, facing them, slowly raising my arms in a gesture of lifting them up, I pray "arise from the dead" to which they all rise. I continue praying "and Christ will give you light" while inviting them to lift their bodies, using their arms and eyes in an upward movement.

Once in awhile, toward the end of class, I will place my hand on each child's head and pray, "May the Lord bless you and keep you. Amen." The times when I have done this most meaningfully is during the last class before Christmas and the last class of the school year.

Some Helps

The best kinds of gestures and movements have their beginning within ourselves and our children. I prepare for this kind of praying by mulling over the words and phrases of a psalm or a song, the invocations of a litany, the words of a prayer or blessing as I am driving or walking, as I'm preparing a meal, as I'm going from store to store in a shopping mall, as I'm waiting at a checkout line in a grocery store, as I'm falling asleep. When I have mulled enough, I involve my whole body in giving expression to the spirit and essence of the prayer. As the movements take shape, I play with them until they are continuous and flowing. Finally, I either write them down or make a quick sketch that shows a picture of the prayer.

Because I want the same kind of prayerful activity to develop in the children I teach, I give them frequent opportunities to mull over and create their own movements as is described above in *Pantomiming*.

I have listed some ways that I use over and over again. There are more and better ways, especially by teachers who are gifted in the art of gesture and movement.

The most important thing is to know and to believe that this is a vital way to pray with children and then to begin doing it. Once you've tasted success and have experienced how quickly most children enter into it, you will pray this way often.

Things to Think About

1. How comfortable are you praying through bodily movement and gesture? What are your favorite prayer movements and gestures?

2. What are your feelings about liturgical dance? Why?

3. How intentionally do you plan into your lessons expressions of prayer through movement, gesture and dance?

Things to Do

1. Contact people in your area who do interpretative or modern dance and ask for help. If a course is available join one for beginners.

2. Read articles or books on dance, gesture and movement. (See the Bibliography at the end of this book.)

3. Experiment on your own. Gesture, gesture, gesture. Dance, dance, dance. Move, move, move. If you begin you will be surprised as your initial stumblings grow into "expressions for feelings that words cannot contain." Using Carla De Sola's description of sacred dance, may what you do alone and with others become both for you and for them "an enfleshment of the spirit in movement to God."

26
Posters and Banners

When I walk into a home, a school, an office, an all-purpose room, a retreat house, a religious education center or a child's room and see posters or banners I spontaneously move toward them to read the words and to study the images. I'm not sure why I find these so attractive or why the inner pull toward them is so great, but I do know that I like them, I remember them easily and they add immensely to the comfort I feel in the place and the people who display them.

I find, too, that I often wonder and chuckle at how well the words and the images give expression to something mysteriously operative at a secret, playful and childlike level of consciousness. For example, my all-time favorite pictures a little raccoon leaning against the bough of a tree, looking straight into the eyes of the viewer. The words on the right as you look at the poster are: "I love to do nothing and then rest afterwards."

I am also frequently fascinated at how the concrete and simple words on a poster or banner say clearly and descriptively what before was, for me, a theological abstraction. For example, "You are the Christ others know best" on a banner in a high school principal's office. Or, these on Argus posters: "There's a ripple effect in all that we do . . . what you do touches me, what I do touches you." "God makes us all alike, yet different." "If the Lord is within, I cannot be without."

I am also always surprised at how children of every age take to banners and posters. Countless times children have unabashedly asked me if I would give them the one I'm using when I don't want it anymore or have asked if I had any other copies of it.

Perhaps my affection for and interest in posters is unique, maybe even addictive, because if I see them in a bookstore or other shop, I will go through the carousel that they are on until I have studied each one. In the gift shops at rest stops along a freeway I have delayed our trips by going through the poster offerings. The Argus posters are sold in many of them.

At home I have a large collection of posters which I like to look at and which I use as prayer and reflection prompters in the spaces where I teach or conduct workshops.

Posters act subliminally on the consciousness of children who see them once in awhile or over a period of time. This was exemplified for me by a fourth grader. In response to the direction, "Draw, in the frame below, a picture that shows what prayer means to you," he drew an image and penned some words that seemed vaguely familiar to me. For a couple of days the image and words haunted me until suddenly I remembered a poster that had been part of the peace movement in the '60s. I showed the child's drawing to his parents who couldn't believe that he had created it. With amazement they told me that they had been active in the peace movement and when he was three years old that poster hung in their home.

As I indicated before, I often display posters in the space where I am teaching, not as a tool specifically referred to, although sometimes I use them that way, too, but as something just there speaking out visually, verbally and silently some of what I hope the children will own in their hearts and minds. If the poster expresses the heart of a unit or the theme of the year, it will frequently be in the space so that its message has time to imprint itself on the children's subconscious as well as their conscious selves. Sometimes a child will ask, "Why?" and I will ask him or her, "What do you think or feel my reasons are?" This usually focuses new attention on it and often another child will explain the poster's meaning, giving it an unsuspected slant. What is perceived in a poster's image and words is somewhat the same and somewhat different for each viewer. Where a poster settles in a child's mind and heart depends on what is going on at the time in his or her inner and outer story.

Ways to Use Posters

There are many other ways in which posters can be used in the development of our children's prayer life.

• Publishers of curriculum materials often create posters to go with their religious education materials. Some of these have prayers on them like the Our Father, the Hail Mary, and the Apostles' Creed. These can be used to introduce the children to these prayers. They can be posted so that the children can see the words while they are praying them. When children are finished with an assignment and have time to spare, seeing the poster may inspire them to pray it spontaneously.

• Posters can also be used as meditation prompters. For example, the one that says simply "Jesus is a Friend of Mine." I place the poster centrally and invite the children to become quiet and to let their eyes rest on the poster. I invite them to think of a friend they have or would like to have. What are some things they do or would do with that friend? What are some things they would say to their friend? What do they think their friend might tell them? Secrets? Sad things? Scary things? Happy things? "Mean things, maybe?" I invite them to think of a time when they made up with a friend after things had gone wrong. Or maybe found a new friend. At this moment I might read to them *A New Friend* by Charlotte Zolotow.

After some quiet moments I refocus them on the poster. Who is always your friend, no matter what you do, no matter what you say, no matter how you are?

We might close our meditation by gathering around the Bible and reading the words about friendship that are part of Jesus' conversation with his disciples at the Last Supper (Jn 15:13-17).

• Posters and banners can also be used to set a tone, to create an atmosphere of quiet, of stillness. For example, "The Lord's quiet is worth listening to." Or, "In silence I hear the voice of God." Or, "When doubts fill my mind, when my heart is in turmoil, quiet me and give me renewed hope and cheer."

• Posters can exercise children's imaginations and encourage wonder and a friendliness to mystery. For example, "Faith is like a rose which unfolds petal by petal." Or "The most beautiful things in the world cannot be seen or even touched. They must be felt with the heart." Or "When God closes one door, He opens another." Or "Can you fathom the mysteries of God? Can you probe the limits of the Almighty?" (Jb 11:7). Or "He tells me that He loves me with every sunrise that He sends." Or "Even I don't always understand me, but God does."

Our faith depends upon a total willingness to accept the truths that are hidden in mystery.

• Banners can teach children what prayer is. For example, "Prayer begins by talking to God, but it ends by listening to Him." Or, "Work a prayer into your life and your day will work out better." Or, "Sing a new song to the Lord" (Ps 96:1).

• Posters can inspire children to compassion. For example, the wonderful one of a small child snuggled up against a little white rabbit above which are the words, "Be Ye Kind" (Eph 4:32). Or "I prayed for justice . . . Then I remembered myself and I prayed for mercy." Or a favorite of mine: A child bent over with his hands lovingly around a little dog who is hurt or sick and the words above say, "No one stands as straight as when he stoops to help someone."

What posters and banners do best and most prayerfully is increase and heighten awareness in a way that creates communion.

Children can make their own banners and posters using pictures and words from magazines, newspapers, literature and the Bible, using materials such as photos, felt, construction paper, scraps of material, crayons, magic markers, colored tissue paper or wrapping paper. If you, your school, or some of the families of your students have computers and the very popular software package *Print Shop* or a similar program, some of the students might find it stimulating to make computerized posters and banners. Often at Christmas time I give the children an opportunity to create mini-banners of the Nativity scene like the one below, which are used as prayer prompters.

• Another prayerful way of involving children in making a banner is to have them first listen to how much God cares for them, even moreso than the flowers of the field, the birds of the air. Then with materials such as those described above they might create individual banners or a group one that shows the things God cares for. Afterwards all gather around their poster and thank God for caring for all things, especially for caring for each of them. This might be concluded with a promise to care for and to respect all created things.

Alternate forms of posters and banners provide interesting possibilities. Each medium used will have its special advantages and limitations, but all will usually combine in some form verbal and visual elements of a single message. Here are a few I've found children of differing ages enjoy.

• *Buttons and badges*, which can be made in a variety of ways from simple cardboard circles to sophisticated photo buttons;

• *Painted rocks*, which have the advantage of making present on a child's desk or table a prayerful expression;

• *Plaques*, made from anything from cardboard to wood, plastic or metal;

• *T-shirts* with sayings and pictures are popular with many young people and can be designed by students in class;

• *Bumper stickers* are popular for their pithy and often humorous messages;

• *Small cards* similar to business cards can be carried in wallet or purse as prayer reminders; and,

• *Cups*, on which are painted brief prayers or prayer-provoking, visual-verbal messages.

Your own creativity and that of your students may come up with even more alternative posters and banners.

When children work together at creating banners and posters, I believe they experience what I call social prayer. Children in my classes have gotten to know each other and have become friends as they talked, created and negotiated the making of a banner or poster. The experience has affected the quality of their lives which might be ultimately what praying is all about.

Things to Think About

1. What are your feelings about posters and banners as prayer helps? What experiences of prayerful banners and posters have you had?

2. What is it about posters and banners that makes them so popular among so many people of widely varying religious backgrounds?

3. What is it about posters and banners that might make them useful helps for prayer in religion class?

Things to Do

1. Since children like banners and posters so much, you might find it helpful to begin your own collection. Keep your eyes open for usable posters and banners as you travel or shop. Many stores from supermarkets to specialty gift shops to highway truck stops to religious goods stores to printing and copy shops offer a great diversity of posters and banners in a wide variety of sizes.

2. To get inside the captivating power of a poster or banner, try making one that conveys one of your own convictions or prayers. Keep the words brief and crisp, possibly with a touch of humor or a twist that the image or images reinforce. Be sure words and visual images relate to create a focused and succinct message. When you finish it, hang it somewhere convenient so you and your family or students may see it, too. Try using it in class as a help for praying.

3. Some bumper stickers have interesting and noteworthy messages. Keep a small notepad in the glove compartment of your car or in your purse and write down those you see and like. Create a banner or poster around the words of one that particularly captures your imagination.

27
Almost Anything

During the summer of 1988 I was teaching a course on Learning Styles at St. Joseph's Seminary in Los Gatos, California. One of the students in my class was Sister Helen Gilsdorf. After I had prayed with the class during the opening class, and had indicated that the following three days I would be dealing with students whose learning preference was aural (second day), visual (third day), and kinesthetic or haptic—touch, experience (fourth day), Sister Helen asked if she could prepare experiences using the ears and eyes for the following two days. Needless to say I was delighted with her offer and looked forward in anticipation to how she would pray with us.

The objects she used to heighten the use of our ears were sea shells and a guitar. To deepen the use of our eyes she used an icon of Jesus and Mary against a cloth that picked up some of the gorgeous gold and burnished colors of the icon. I barely remember the words we sang and prayed on both of those days but the objects are imbedded in both my conscious and unconscious memory. Perhaps it is the child in me, but I was fascinated with the large seashell and delighted with her invitation to us to pick it up during the day and to listen to the sounds within. I found myself spontaneously listening not just to the seashell but to thoughts and words within myself.

The icon was so beautiful that its image is etched in my memory and I am considering purchasing one similar to it so that I might pray more with my eyes and, also, to have it available for prayer with the children I teach.

Almost anything can be used for prayer. It takes some imagination and time to use objects meaningfully and prayerfully, but they can unleash in pray-ers wonder, fascination, awe, praise, joy, playfulness, reverence and delight.

A flower, a plant, a leaf, a rock, a loaf of bread, a glass of water, a candle, clay, aluminum foil, a statue, a piece of sculpture, a rosary or a cross are just a few of the objects that can be part of our prayer with children or adults.

174

Some Helpful Hints

I have used a wide variety of things in my own prayer and in my classes with children. Here are some suggestions I have regarding the use of objects in prayer experiences.

Page through books of celebrations for children, such as *Liturgies for Little Ones* by Carol Rezy (Ave Maria Press) for ideas. There are all kinds of wonderful things suggested in the part of the celebration designated "Preparation of Gifts." For example, a ball of clay and some things made of clay, a straw basket of construction-paper flowers, a picture of a family, a globe, a collage containing the children's pictures, Halloween masks, mirrors, clocks, a cardboard door with the words "Knock and the door will be opened to you," baskets of food and clothes, sandals and sheepskin, a crib with baby Jesus inside, newspaper, a fishing pole, band-aids, a shamrock, lilies, an Easter basket, a vestment, a beach ball, bread, water and wine.

Once you have selected an object, spend time before class with the object in relation to prayer to discern if and how it fits, if it adds a dimension that the words of a prayer don't, if it captures your imagination. Does gazing at it or holding it or listening to it cause something to happen *within* you? Objects need to distract as well as focus. By *distract* I mean cause you to get lost in it enough so that a richer meaning unfolds quietly and interiorly.

Use fewer objects rather than more within a given prayer experience. As a rule I favor one, but one that deepens what is already a part of the whole.

Using the same object in more than one prayer experience during the year is desirable. For example, using the same icon of Mary in prayers that honor her can deepen her impression on the heart, mind and spirit.

Focus the children's attention on the object at the beginning of the prayer or during it. Or, suggest that they do something with the object as the prayer progresses.

An object need not be used as part of every class's prayer. "Once in awhile" is a good rule of thumb.

On occasion, especially with older children, suggest that one or other of the students look at the prayer or the psalm verse for a succeeding class and choose an object and a form for praying with it and the words.

On occasion, too, invite the children to form an object, create a shape while silently thinking about God, about prayer. For example, place a 12" square of aluminum foil on the table or desk by each child. Invite them to take the piece of foil in their hands and hold it doing nothing with it—just becoming quiet. Then direct them to put their minds on God and prayer and to begin molding the foil into a shape that says who God is for them or what prayer is. Say nothing more—pray in the same way yourself with a piece of foil. After several moments, invite the children to describe their shapes or to pray with them. You might begin with yours or do yours at the end.

On special occasions give each child a miniature of the object that is part of your prayer. For example, if a cross is used during a Lenten prayer, give each child a small wooden cross to carry in his or her pocket. Or, if an art masterpiece is used, give each child a postcard size copy of it.

The value of various common or unusual objects is that they bring into play more of the children's senses—seeing and touching and smelling as well as hearing. They spark the imagination, sometimes surprise or pose questions, foster wonder and provide a focus—all helpful for prayer.

I want to share with you a moving story that reveals the power of a very common object for both teaching and praying when used by a sensitive, creative catechist with sensitive, creative students. It is the story of Philip, a true story by Harry Pritchett, Jr.

Once upon a time I had a young friend named Philip. Philip lived in a nearby city and Philip was born a mongoloid. He was a pleasant child—happy it seemed—but increasingly aware of the difference between himself and other children.

Philip went to Sunday school. And his teacher, also, was a friend of mine. My Sunday school teacher friend taught the third grade at a Methodist Church. Philip was in his class, as well as nine other 8-year-old boys and girls.

My Sunday school teacher friend is a very creative teacher. Most of you know 8-year-olds. And Philip with his differences was not readily accepted as a member of this third grade Sunday school class. But my teacher friend was a good teacher and he helped facilitate a good group of 8-year-old children. They learned and they laughed and they played together. And they really cared about each other—even though, as you know, 8-year-olds don't say that they care about each other out loud very often. But my teacher friend could see it. He knew it. He also knew that Philip was not really a part of that group of children. Philip, of course, did not choose nor did he want to be different. He just was. And that was the way things were.

My Sunday school teacher friend had a marvelous design for his class on the Sunday after Easter last year. You know those things that panty hose come in—the containers that look like big eggs. My friend had collected ten of those to use on that Sunday. The children loved it when he brought them into the room. Each child was to get a great big egg. It was a beautiful Spring day and the assigned task was for each child to go outside on the church grounds and to find a symbol for new life, put it into the egg, and bring it back into the classroom. They would mix them all up and then open and share their new-life symbols and surprises all together one by one.

Well, they did this and it was glorious. And it was confusing. And it was wild. They ran all around gathering their symbols and returned to the classroom. They put all the big eggs on a table and then my teacher friend began to open them. All the children were standing around the table. He opened one and there was a flower. They oohed and aahed. He opened another and there was a little butterfly. "Beautiful!" said the girls, since it is very hard for 8-year-old boys to say "Beautiful!"

He opened another and there was a rock. And as third graders will, some laughed, and some said, "That's crazy! How's a rock supposed to be like new life?" But the smart little boy whose egg they had spoken of spoke up. He said, "That's mine. And I knew that all of you would get flowers and buds and leaves and butterflies and stuff like that. So I got a rock because I wanted to be different. And for me, that's new life!" They all laughed. My teacher friend said something to himself about the profundity of 8-year-olds and went on opening the egg surprises.

He opened the next one and there was nothing there. The other children, as 8-

year-olds will, said, "That's not fair!" "That's stupid!" "Somebody didn't do it right!" About that time my teacher friend felt a tug on his shirt and he looked down and Philip was standing there.

"It's mine!" Philip said. "That's mine!" And the children said, "You don't ever do things right, Philip. There's nothing there!" "I did so do it," Philip said. "I did do it. It's empty—the tomb is empty!"

The class was silent, a very full silence. And for you people who don't believe in miracles, I want to tell you that one happened that day last Spring. From that time on, it was different. Philip suddenly became a part of that group of 8-year-old children. They took him in. He entered. He was set free from the tomb of his differentness.

Philip died last summer. His family had known since the time that he was born that he wouldn't live out a full life span. Many other things had been wrong with his tiny little body. And so, late last July, with an infection that most normal children could have quickly shrugged off, Philip died. The mystery simply enveloped him completely.

He was buried from that church. And on that day, at that funeral, nine 8-year-old children marched right up to that altar—not with flowers to cover the stark reality of death. Nine 8-year-olds, with their Sunday school teacher, marched right up to that altar and lay on it an empty egg—an empty old discarded holder of panty hose.

Few stories I know show—among other things—the potential of ordinary, commonplace objects when used creatively for prayer. A number of parishes where I shared this story centered part of their Easter celebration around Philip and his empty egg.

Paul says in his letter to the Colossians that in Christ "were created all things in heaven and on earth, the visible, and invisible. / . . . all things were created through him and for him. / . . . In him all things hold together" (Col 1:16-17). Catholic Christians believe, then, that all things can help us meet Christ in our lives. The church's whole sacramental system is built on that belief. All creation is a sacrament, a potential meeting place with the Lord. So the church has from the beginning made use of many commonplace objects for public and private prayer. We catechists can extend that down-to-earth approach to prayer in the classroom as well.

Things to Think About

1. What objects, natural or man-made, have you found helpful in your own prayer? in your classes?

2. How do you feel about using things like discarded egg-shaped panty-hose containers (or other ordinary things) for prayer?

3. What keeps you and other catechists from making use of the limitless resource of things to help yourself and children pray?

Things to Do

1. Select some object you normally would not think of as a help for personal prayer or for helping children in class learn to pray. Take some time to pray with it yourself. Then plan how you will use it with the children in one of your upcoming classes.

2. Find a quiet quarter hour when you will not be disturbed. Take a sheet of aluminum foil. Become aware of God's presence with you. Slowly, as a prayer, shape the foil into whatever shape suggests how you feel about yourself before God. Hold up the completed sculpture, offering yourself to God.

3. Begin a collection of objects you would like to use for your own prayer or with children. Gradually collect things that strike you as useful for prayer. Slowly you will have built up a rich prayer resource for yourself and your students.

28
Spontaneous Prayers

I heard a Protestant Navy chaplain tell of a time when he was in a dangerous and frightening situation. The prayer that came to him spontaneously was one that he had learned in Sunday School.

Jesus loves me
This I know
Because the Bible
Tells me so.

He chuckled about the memory as he was sharing it with us. He also told us that he still wonders why that was the only prayer out of a lifetime of praying that surfaced at a time of almost mortal danger.

There are many kinds of spontaneous prayers. One kind are those that bubble up to the surface of our consciousness when we need them, such as the one above prayed by the chaplain.

His experience brings to mind a similar experience told by Herb Montgomery in his beautiful book, *The Splendor of the Psalms*. He recalls being hospitalized once in a foreign country. Far from home and family he was both sick and lonely. He found himself praying the first words of Psalm 23: "The Lord is my shepherd; I shall not want." He thanks a teacher years before who had him and his classmates memorize those words.

As I mentioned earlier, in the chapter on scripture, I have often experienced this spontaneous surfacing of previously memorized prayers in the most varied and unexpected situations.

The kind of spontaneous prayer described by the chaplain, by Herb Montgomery and by myself, is comfortable for most Catholics. The spontaneity rests in the unpredictable bubbling to the surface of prayers once learned by heart.

179

But, for most catechists and parents who grew up before truly spontaneous prayer became common among Catholics, mostly after Vatican Council II in the 1960s, being expected to pray without a fixed formula, especially in public, can be a disconcerting, even frightening experience.

Younger Catholics are often much more at home with spontaneous prayer because it is part of most religion classes, and also many families pray spontaneously in their homes. If a catechist or a parent is comfortable with spontaneous prayer and models it for the children, they tend to take to it rather easily, except for individuals who may be excessively shy or anxious.

Genuinely spontaneous prayers are the result of growing up with attitudes toward life described in earlier chapters: looking for God in all things, openness, thankfulness, reverence, compassion. These attitudes grow normally from being with prayerful people, who pray almost any time and any place. Adults who often find themselves praying spontaneously are usually people who grew up praying, although there are many adults who only started praying when they were grown up.

Be that as it may, I feel strongly my responsibility as a catechist to develop in children a sense that God's care and God's help are only a prayer away.

Many Kinds of Spontaneous Prayer

In addition to the unpremeditated bubbling up of previously learned prayers, a variety of prayers can be called spontaneous prayer.

One of the most common and yet most frightening for some is the kind that we pray on the spot, so to speak, at the invitation of another for some special occasion. For example, a host or hostess without warning asks a guest to grace a meal with prayer. Instinctively some Catholics handle the situation by simply reciting a traditional Grace at Meals. Others will pray with words tailored to the occasion for the meal, taking special note of those who are gathered around the table.

Spontaneous prayers are also as simple as the adding of a person's name or intention during the Prayers of the Faithful at Mass. Or, a bit more challenging, making up intercessions themselves on the spot.

Still other kinds of spontaneous prayers are those that are written by children or adults in a daily journal. Journal writers often find that the process of writing about daily events and feelings quite naturally moves into moments of unplanned prayer.

Yet another kind of spontaneous prayer is one that we pray in admiration of a beautiful sunset, a bouquet of flowers, a natural wonder like the Grand Canyon or that we utter in thanksgiving when something turns out well or when someone is found who was lost or when news is not as bad as we were sure it was going to be. Or when we are in a new, challenging or frightening situation and we hear ourselves praying words like, "Lord, help me get through this." Or when we are conscious that we have sinned, made a stupid decision, or even accidently done something that hurts another, we find ourselves praying to God for forgiveness and mercy.

What can catechists do with children to nurture in them the possibility of a lifetime in which these kinds of spontaneous praying are natural and habitual?

How to Foster Spontaneous Prayer in Children

I do everything I can to bring my students together with a great variety of prayer, especially the psalms, and to encourage them to learn as many as possible by heart. My hope is that these prayers, in their minds and hearts, will be a source of comfort, encouragement, peace and strength throughout their lives, and will provide a rich source of prayer upon which to draw in praying spontaneously.

Besides having children learn as many prayers as possible by heart so that prayers are available to them at any and all times, there are other ways in which children can grow in the art of praying spontaneously. Here are some examples:

• *Semi-structured dialogue.*   I involve the children in prayer experiences in which dialogues between them and God, Jesus, Mary, a saint are structured in, but the content of the dialogue remains open. Such a prayer in class might go something like this:

> Jesus: "I tried to tell you something last night but you seemed really preoccupied."
> Child: responds with whatever he or she wants to say.
> Jesus: says something back.
> Child: responds again.
> Jesus: speaks again.
> Child: answers.

At times the child has the last word, which is often a statement of praise, or thanks, or petition, or regret and resolution. At other times Jesus or God or Mary or the saint has the last word, which often is a promise or reminder that they are never alone, that they can do it, that they are special and precious. Depending on the age of the students the conversations can be shorter or longer and they can be about anything.

Sometimes the children have kept their conversations in a notebook and I have encouraged them to do this kind of dialoguing on their own.

• *Litanies.*   Making up litanies is another way of praying spontaneously and easily, which provides a kind of format or structure for spontaneous prayer. I gradually introduce the children to one or two litanies, like the "Litany of the Blessed Virgin" or the "Litany of the Saints." Once they are familiar with what a litany is and how it is put together, I invite them to pray spontaneous litanies.

The litany can be an expression of appreciation for things that God has done, like making them so special, and the refrain, "We thank you, God." Or, it can be a prayer of invoking the names of saints and Christian heroes with the refrain "Pray for us." Or, a litany of promise such as "When I see someone who is lonely . . ." and the refrain, "I will show I care, Jesus."

• *General Intercessions at Mass.*   I do the same thing with the General Intercessions of the Mass. First I share with the students one or more formulations of these prayers, also known as the Prayers of the Faithful. Most of the children are passively familiar with them from their attendance at Mass, but few have reflected on the basic structure which consists of the announcement to the community of someone or something to pray for, followed by the repeated community intercession that God respond to the expressed need or petition. The students are even less aware of the general pattern of these General Intercessions, namely that they move in a fairly predictable sequence:

—for the needs of the church,

—for public authorities and the salvation of the world,

—for those oppressed by any need,

—for the local community.

Once the students are sufficiently familiar with the structure and sequence of these liturgical prayers, I invite them to pray for people and things that are of particular concern for them. The structure and pattern of these prayers may then be reinforced whenever they participate in the Sunday Eucharist. They will also have a sense that our prayers, especially of petition, are to be more all-embracing than merely our personal needs and desires. As Catholic Christians we are called to reach out in prayer to the whole world as well as to the whole church.

• *Other liturgical prayers.*   Similarly, other liturgical prayers provide a rather predictable format for prayer while allowing free personal expression. Becoming comfortable with the format can free youngsters to pray spontaneously within that format. For example, the Opening Prayer of the Eucharist reveals a general pattern that can facilitate spontaneous praying. Here is the one for the Sixth Sunday in Ordinary Time.

> Address to God
> > *God, our Father,*
> Something God has done for us that grounds our present petition
> > *you have promised to remain forever with those who do what is just and right.*
> The petition itself
> > *Help us to live in your presence.*
> The person(s) through whom we pray.
> > *We ask this through our Lord, Jesus Christ,*
> > *your Son,*
> > *who lives and reigns with you*
> > *and the Holy Spirit,*
> > *one God, for ever and ever.*

The overall pattern of liturgical prayer is *to* the Father, *through* the Son *in* the Holy Spirit.

Another form of liturgical prayer that provides a pattern for spontaneous prayer is that of *blessing*, which generally follows the same pattern as the Opening Prayer of the eucharistic liturgy. For example the blessing proposed by the American bishops for blessing the kitchen of a new home:

> O God,
> you fill the hungry with good things.
> Send your blessing on us, as we work in this kitchen,
> and make us ever thankful for our daily bread.
> Grant this, through Christ our Lord.

• *Creating prayers* in which the children have a single word like *praise, love, believe, hope, thanks* and *please* to work with allows them to ground their prayer in a fundamental prayer expression, while leaving open the exact words. The psalms, for example, center on a number of major themes like those mentioned above, but these central biblical themes find rich and exciting variations in the 150 psalms.

Sometimes I have had the children take the new words that are part of their lesson and create a prayer with them.

• *Association.*   Another way to get children praying spontaneously is for you to begin a prayer that connects with something that is going on in the community and inviting them to add to it. For example, after a synagogue in our area was defaced and we had reflected on the prejudice and vandalism involved using a worksheet, I invited them to pray, telling them that I would start the prayer and they were to continue it with their own feelings and sentiments. I began by praying, "O God, I am sorry that one of your houses in our neighborhood was vandalized and I ask forgiveness for the young people who did it." One of the children prayed, "God, I'm mad about what has happened to the synagogue—maybe you need to forgive me for my anger." Another child prayed, "Bless the people who are hurt because their prayerhouse was hurt." And still another prayed, "Take care of Rabbi Laszlo Berkowits and all the people who worship at Temple Rodef Shalom."

In connection with learning about the commandments, or the beatitudes, children might pray spontaneously asking for help in being truthful, in being respectful of the property of others, in resisting temptation to steal, in doing what their parents ask them to do, in reaching out in justice to those who are poor and needy.

Since one traditional definition of prayer is talking to God, anything that a child talks to God about could rightly be considered spontaneous prayer. The important thing is to help children make their own the truth that God's help and care are only a prayer away.

Things to Think About

1. What has been your experience with spontaneous prayer in your own life? What do you feel helped or hindered your growth in praying spontaneously?

2. In what situations do you find yourself most often praying spontaneously?

3. What ways have you found effective in helping your students become familiar with spontaneous prayer?

Things to Do

1. It can be helpful on occasion to jot down prayers that arise spontaneously in your heart and on your lips. Becoming more conscious of your preferred spontaneous prayers may be useful in deepening your appreciation of those very prayers through other methods of prayer. For example, take one of your common spontaneous prayers as the subject of several minutes meditation. Pray it word for word, slowly, pondering the meaning of each word as long as you find it fruitful. Or, if it is a biblical prayer, look it up in the Bible and consider its meaning in its context in the Bible.

2. Liturgical prayers sometimes provide helpful formats or patterns for spontaneous prayers. Become familiar with the format for the eucharistic liturgy's Opening Prayer and blessings, for example. Then each day for a week, perhaps as morning and evening prayers, or before class or work or a social event, pray a spontaneous prayer suitable to the occasion but following the liturgical prayer's structure. In this way you will become comfortable with a simple prayer format that you may fill in for use in many different situations.

3. Reflect on how many prayers you have had your students learn by heart. Determine to have them memorize some new prayer, even if it be just a brief psalm verse, each week or two. Select the prayers for them or invite them to find meaningful prayers that they would like to learn by heart.

An After Thought

As the writing of this book is reaching its final stages I am having some second or after thoughts. Did I leave out an aspect of prayer without which no book on prayer should be written? Did I tell too much of my own story of praying with children? Did I go into too much detail? Will the suggestions, the reflections on "how to," make the effort too complicated, too time-consuming and therefore hinder rather than help? Is there unnecessary repetition? Only you the reader-user will be able to answer these and other unasked questions that are plaguing me at this point.

The only way I seem able to let go and let be is to add here a poem that was given to me as a gift. I do not know who the author is nor did the person who gave it to me know the source. Therefore I am unable to credit it, but I will do so in a later printing should its author become known. It somehow expresses perfectly what I'm feeling now and what I often feel about prayer.

TEACHING PRAYER

I do not much trust those who speak easily of prayer,
    or who quickly enter any sacred place.
For I am ill at ease with all who are
    on casual terms with beauty
    unfrightened by truth
    without terror in the face of love.
I am not inclined to believe anyone who can
    translate silence into words,
    blueprint mystery,
    describe relationships,
    tell you how it is to meet someone,
    make surrender believable,
    read aloud love letters without laughing.
Excuse me please,
    and these words spoken on the way to silence
    for though we stutter at its edge,
    and give tongue-tied praise,
    we know it to be heard.

Bibliography

Scripture

Brokamp, Sister Marilyn. *Psalms for Children*. Cincinnati, OH: St. Anthony Messenger Press, 1982.

Carwell, L. Ann. *The Good Shepherd Prayer: Understanding the 23rd Psalm*. St. Louis, MO: Concordia Publishing House, 1979.

Gallagher, Maureen, Clare Wagner and David Woeste. *Praying With Scripture*. Mahwah, NJ: Paulist Press, 1983.

Glavich, Sr. Mary Kathleen, SND. *Acting Out the Miracles and Parables: 52 Five-Minute Plays for Education and Worship*. Mystic, CT: Twenty-Third Publications, 1988.

Montgomery, Herb and Mary. *The Splendor of the Psalms*. San Francisco, CA: Harper & Row, 1977.

Mullaly, Larry. *The Golden Link: Gospel Playlets for Schools and Parish Liturgies*. San Jose, CA: Resource Publications, Inc., 1985.

Reehorst, Jane. *Guided Meditations for Children: How to Teach Children to Pray Using Scripture*. Dubuque, IA: Wm. C. Brown, 1986.

Short, Beth. *Memorizing Bible Verses with Games & Crafts*. St. Louis, MO: Concordia Publishing House, 1984.

Prayer Services and Liturgical Celebrations

Cronin, Gaynell Bordes. *Holy Days and Holidays: Prayer Celebrations With Children* (2 volumes). San Francisco: Harper & Row, 1985, 1988.

Eitzen, Ruth. *Fun to Do All Year Through*. Valley Forge, PA: Judson Press, 1982.

Halmo, Joan. *Celebrating the Church Year With Young Children*. Collegeville, MN: The Liturgical Press, 1988.

Machado, Mary Kathryn. *How to Plan Children's Liturgies*. San Jose, CA: Resource Publications, Inc., 1985.

Mathson, Patricia. *Pray & Play: 28 Prayer Services and Activities for Children in K Through Sixth Grade*. Notre Dame, IN: Ave Maria Press, 1989.

Rezy, Carol. *Liturgies for Little Ones: 38 Celebrations for Grades One to Three*. Notre Dame, IN: Ave Maria Press, 1978.

Traditional and Spontaneous Prayer

Bannon, J.F., R. Burke, J.F. Gough, B. Halpin, E. MacLochain. *Prayer Forms: Twenty-Two Prayer Forms for Classrooms & Youth Groups*. Mystic, CT: Twenty-Third Publications, 1985.

Brokamp, Marilyn. *Prayer Times for Primary Grades*. Cincinnati, OH: St. Anthony Messenger Press, 1987.

Caprio, Betsy. *Experiments in Prayer*. Notre Dame, IN: Ave Maria Press, 1973.

Costello, Gwen. *Stations of the Cross for Teenagers*. Mystic, CT: Twenty-Third Publications, 1988.

Darcy-Berube, Francoise and John Paul Berube. *Someone's There: Paths to Prayer for Young People*. Notre Dame, IN: Ave Maria Press, 1986.

Donze, Mary Terese. *Prayer and Our Children*. Notre Dame, IN: Ave Maria Press, 1987.

_____. *In My Heart Room: 16 Love Prayers for Little Children*. Liguori, MO: Liguori Publications, 1982.

Gompertz, Helen. *My Book of Prayers*. Valley Forge, PA: Judson Press, 1986.

Halpin, Marlene. *Puddles of Knowing*. Dubuque, IA: Wm. C. Brown, 1984.

Hein, Lucille E. *I Can Make My Own Prayers*. Valley Forge, PA: Judson Press, 1971.

_____. *Thank You, God*. Valley Forge, PA: Judson Press, 1981.

Hesch, John B. *Prayer & Meditation for Middle School Kids*. Mahwah, NJ: Paulist Press, 1985.

Nouwen, Henri. *Behold the Beauty of the Lord: Praying With Icons*. Notre Dame, IN: Ave Maria Press, 1987.

Pfeifer, Carl and Janaan Manternach. *Living Water: Prayers of Our Heritage*. Mahwah, NJ: Paulist Press, 1978.

Puig, Enric. *Lord, I Am One of Your Little Ones: Prayers for Children*. Chicago: Loyola University Press, 1987.

Savary, Louis, ed. *The Rosary for Children*. New York: The Regina Press, 1980.

Schreivogel, Paul A. and George Ellen Hohngren, CSJ. *Small Prayers for Small Children About Big and Little Things*. Minneapolis, MN: Augsburg Publishing House, 1980.

Shea, John. *The God Who Fell From Heaven*. Valencia, CA: Tabor Publishing, 1979.

Simons, Thomas G. *Blessings for God's People*. Notre Dame, IN: Ave Maria Press, 1983.

Skelly, Sister Maureen. *Lord, Do You Hear Me?* New York: The Regina Press, 1986.

Winter, Art, ed. *Praying* (a bi-monthly journal). Kansas City, MO: National Catholic Reporter.

Family and Prayer

Bishops' Committee on the Liturgy, National Conference of Catholic Bishops. *Catholic Household Blessings & Prayers*. Washington, DC: United States Catholic Conference, Inc., 1988.

De Gidio, Sandra. *Enriching Faith Through Family Celebrations*. Mystic, CT: Twenty-Third Publications, 1989.

Huck, Gabe. *Book of Family Prayer*. San Franciso, CA: Harper & Row, 1979.

_____. *Table Prayer Book*. Chicago: Liturgy Training Publications, 1979.

Jasper, Tony, ed. *The Illustrated Family Prayer Book*. San Francisco, CA: Harper and Row, 1981.

Shenk, Sara Wenger. *Why Not Celebrate?* Intercourse, PA: Good Books, 1987.

Sherrer, Quin. *How to Pray for Your Children*. Lynnwood, WA: Aglow Publications, 1986.

Travnikar, Rock. *The Blessing Cup*. Cincinnati, OH: St. Anthony Messenger Press, 1979.

Stories and Poetry

Bang, Molly. *The Paper Crane*. New York: Morrow (Greenwillow Books), 1985.

Baylor, Byrd. *The Way to Start a Day*. New York: Macmillan (Charles Scribner's Sons), 1978.

Beckmann, Beverly Ann. *From: Understanding the Resurrection*. St. Louis, MO: Concordia Publishing House, 1980.

Bitney, James & Suzanne Schaffhausen. *Sunday's Children: Prayers in the Language of Children.* San Jose, CA: Resource Publications, 1986.

Brown, Marcia. *Stone Soup.* New York: Macmillan (Scribner), 1947.

Brown, Margaret Wise. *The Runaway Bunny.* New York: Harper & Row (Trophy Picture Books), 1977.

Cohen, Barbara. *Yussel's Prayer.* New York: Lothrop, Lee & Shepard, 1981.

De Gasztold, Carmen Bernos. Rumer Godden, trans. *Prayers From the Ark* and *The Creatures Choir.* New York: The Viking Press (Penguin Books), 1976.

De Paola, Tomie. *The Legend of the Bluebonnet.* New York: Putnam Publishing Group, 1983.

Flournoy, Valerie. *The Patchwork Quilt.* New York: E. P. Dutton, 1985.

Freedman, Florence B. *Brothers: A Hebrew Legend.* New York: Harper & Row, 1985.

Goffstein, M. B. *An Artist.* New York: Harper & Row, 1980.

———. *My Noah's Ark.* New York: Harper & Row, 1978.

———. *Natural History.* New York: Farrar, Strauss & Giroux, 1979.

———. *Our Snowman.* New York: Harper & Row, 1986.

Heide, Florence Parry. *I Love Every People.* St. Louis, MO: Concordia Publishing House, 1978.

Hopkins, Lee Bennett. *Pass the Poetry, Please!* New York: Harper & Row, 1987.

Juknialis, Joseph J. *Angels to Wish By: A Book of Story Prayers.* San Jose, CA: Resource Publications, 1984.

Kenneally, Christy. *Miracles and Me: Poems for Children.* Mahwah, NJ: Paulist Press, 1986.

———. *Strings and Things: Poems and Other Messages for Children.* Mahwah, NJ: Paulist Press, 1984.

Larrick, Nancy. *Tambourines! Tambourines to Glory! Prayers and Poems.* Philadelphia, PA: Westminster John Knox Press, 1982.

Lionni, Leo. *It's Mine.* New York: Alfred A. Knopf, 1986.

———. *Little Blue and Little Yellow.* New York: Ivan Obolensky, 1979.

———. *Tico and the Golden Wings.* New York: Alfred A. Knopf, 1987.

Munsch, Robert. *Love You Forever.* Scarborough, Ontario, Canada: Firefly Books, Ltd., 1988.

Murphy, Elspeth Campbell. *David and I Talk to God: Psalms for Children* series and *God's Words in My Heart* series. Elgin, IL: David C. Cook.

Nixon, Joan Lowery. *The Butterfly Tree.* Huntington, IN: Our Sunday Visitor, 1979.

Pottebaum, Gerard A. *The Festival of Art.* Minneapolis, MN: Augsburg Publishing House, 1971.

Rylant, Cynthia. *Every Living Thing.* New York: Macmillan (Aladdin Books), 1988.

Silverstein, Shel. *The Giving Tree.* New York: Harper & Row, 1964.

Steptoe, John. *The Story of Jumping Mouse.* New York: Lothrop, Lee & Shepard, 1984.

Stevenson, Rosemarie. *A Day to Pray: A Collection of Poems, Prayers and Praise.* Melbourne, Australia: The Joint Board of Christian Education, 1988.

Tolstoy, Leo. *Papa Panov's Special Day.* Batavia, IL: Lion Publishing Corporation, 1988.

Movement, Gesture, Dance

De Sola, Carla. *Learning Through Dance*. Austin, TX: The Sharing Company, 1974.

_____. *The Spirit Moves: A Handbook of Dance and Prayer*. Washington, DC: The Liturgical Conference, 1977.

Dietering, Carolyn. *Actions, Gestures & Bodily Attitudes*. San Jose, CA: Resource Publications, 1980.

Ortegel, Sister Adelaide. *A Dancing People*. Berkeley, CA: Sacred Dance Guild, 1976.

Banners, Posters and Pictures

Argus Posters. P. O. Box 7000, Allen, TX 75002.

Atwood, Corey. *Banners for Beginners*. Wilton, CT: Morehouse, Barlow, 1987.

Judson, Sylvia Shaw. *The Quiet Eye*. Chicago, IL: Regnery Gateway, 1982.

Knuth, Jill. *Banners Without Words*. San Jose, CA: Resource Publications, Inc., 1985.

Scharper, Philip and Sally, eds. *The Gospel in Art by the Peasants of Solentiname*. Maryknoll, NY: Orbis Books, 1984.